Talking with Jesus

Evelyn Klumpenhouwer

Talking with Jesus

Published by
Communion with God Ministries
www.CWGMinistries.org
ISBN 1 86263 019 4
Printed in the United States of America

COMMUNION WITH GOD
M I N I S T R I E S
Not studies about God,
but encounters with God.

Dedication

This book is dedicated to my Lord Jesus Christ "How precious also are thy thoughts unto me, **O** God! how great is the sum of them!"

&

To My Husband Ben
for daily encouraging me with his love and prayers
"I Love You"

Table of Contents

Foreword

Talking with Jesus! How exciting! How awesome! Is it really possible in the 20th century? We know Adam and Eve talked with God, and the 12 disciples walked and talked with Jesus, but is it still possible today to dialogue with Jesus?

This book demonstrates that, "Yes" it is! It is possible to hear the Master's voice. It is possible to be led by both His written and spoken word. Christ's death tore the veil from top to bottom so that all of mankind could come and commune with the Father. In this book you will experience the lovely, and powerful words of our Lord and Savior as He speaks through both His written and spoken words. You will find a year of devotional study, as you hear His heartfelt love reaching out to you, touching you and healing you. Jesus said, "My words are life." You will be saturated with His life as you devour His words in the pages that follow.

I thank Evelyn Klumpenhouwer for taking the time to record and share with all of us the beauty of her inner walk with the Master. It is a gift that I and many others will treasure for years to come. Thank you Evelyn.

But now in turning to you the reader. Maybe you can't hear His voice in the midst of your heart. Maybe you can't record the beautiful loving, healing words He is speaking within you. There was a day that I couldn't. However the Lord answered my heart's cry by having me invest a year of my life into learning to discern His voice. That year He taught me four simple keys that unlocked the door to two-way prayer.

I have taught those keys to over 1 million people and found that all who apply them find that they too can begin to write and record the words the Lord is speaking within their hearts. It is not hard. One simply must become like a child, and understand the simply basics of experiencing God in the Spirit World. I teach these four keys in my book, *Dialogue With God*, which is made available at the close of this book. If you need help in learning to hear and record your dialogue with Jesus, I encourage you to avail yourself of this book.

It is not often that the writer of a forward recommends another book along with the one he is writing the forward for. However Evelyn herself says that the principles taught in *Dialogue With God* were what allowed her to begin writing her own dialogue with Jesus. Therefore, for many these books will go hand in hand, bringing them into a whole new place of spiritual intimacy with their Lord and Savior Jesus Christ.

I believe *Talking With Jesus* is the beginning of a vast array of books which will demonstrate in many ways that man truly can have ongoing intimacy with their Lord and Creator, Jesus Christ. I give this book my highest recommendation, and shall find myself feasting on its pages for years to come. Take it and share it with a friend.

Mark Virkler

About The Author...

Evelyn Klumpenhouwer and her husband Ben lived in Athens, Ontario. They have retired from pastoring a local church and Evelyn has now received her eternal reward and gone on to be with her Lord. Their family includes three married children, twelve grandchildren and one great grandchild, all loving the Lord. Hearing the Lord speaking to them has been very important in all of their lives.

Born March 13, 1943, in Holland, Evelyn immigrated with her parents to Canada in June 1952. In March 1963 she married her husband Ben. Together they were involved in a counselling ministry and Evelyn did some teaching in their local church.

"I have been journaling since Jan. 9, 1986, when I attended a "Communion With God" seminar held by Rev. Mark Virkler. This course has truly enriched my relationship with God. Since that time I have had the opportunity to share and teach this course in our local church, Maranatha Christian Fellowship Church, Brockville, Ontario."

JANUARY 1

Daily Reading: Proverbs 3

Proverbs 3:26 *For the Lord shall be thy confidence, and shall keep thy foot from being taken.*

I love you. I see your heart is filled with expectation for the new year, but I also see fears and doubts. My child do not fear and doubt. My heart breaks when I see you give expression to those fears and doubts. Has My way not always been the best way? Trust Me completely. My word declares that the King's heart is in My hand and I can turn it wherever I want. So trust Me completely to do what is best for you. This will be a good year and I will bless you abundantly. Rejoice more in Me and when you feel a strain start rejoicing. Your expectations shall not be cut off.

JANUARY 2

Daily Reading: Genesis 3

Genesis 3:9 *And the Lord God called unto Adam, and said unto him, Where art thou?*

My child, I love you. You are a delight to Me. I enjoy this time of communion and fellowship with you.

Every day I sought out Adam in the garden of Eden and we had a sweet time of fellowship. We shared the day's happenings with one another, but sin came into the picture and the first thing that happened was that Adam hid from Me. He was afraid to have fellowship with Me.

Many times when you do not seek Me for fellowship or communion it is because sin has entered the picture and you draw away from Me.

I love you so much and it brings so much joy and happiness to My heart when you seek My fellowship.

JANUARY 3

Daily Reading: Matthew 4:17-25

Matthew 4:19   *And He saith unto them, Follow Me, and I will make you fishers of men.*

My son and my daughter, I am with you. I am ever before you. I have set before you goals. I will bring to pass the goals that I have given you, for they are My promises to you.

Not one word of My promises has ever failed to come to pass. You should always keep these goals before you, but I am the one who makes it happen. Fasten your eyes on Me, the author and finisher of all these promises and goals.

Commit all things to Me and lean not to your own understanding. Not everyone will be able to understand this, as they can only see the present with its immediate problems. They too must look to Me for I am their answer also; the solution to their immediate problem.

Cast all your cares on Me and I will sustain you, help you and love you.

JANUARY 4

Daily Reading: Exodus 1:15-22, 2:1-10

Psalm 91;10,11   *There shall no evil befall thee, neither shall any plague come nigh thy dwelling. For He shall give His angels charge over thee, to keep thee in all thy ways.*

Rejoice in thanksgiving, though a host should encamp against you (and they have), I the Lord have been victorious. I have defeated the enemy. He put out snares to trap you, to bring you low and to destroy you, but I came to your rescue.

I love you and I have set my angels to watch over you and keep you in all your ways. Do not retreat, but go full force ahead. I have given you the victory. Praise Me, rejoice in Me and in My power and glory. Have a glorious and rejoicing day. I am the Lord YOUR God and I love you.

JANUARY 5

Daily Reading: Exodus 33:8-17

John 15:15   *Henceforth I call you not servants; for the servant knoweth not what his lord doeth: but I have called you friends; for all things that I have heard of My Father I have made known unto you.*

I am pleased that you have set this time apart to spend with Me. It is easier for you to hear My voice when you are listening for it. There is so much I want to share with My people.

I had communion daily with Adam in the garden. Abraham was My friend; we had fellowship together. My word declares that I desire fellowship and communion with all My people.

Do not let this time slide for it is precious. I desire for you to have a channel through which we can communicate.

Do not fear the days ahead, for I am going before you and preparing the way. Continue to seek My protection and come against the enemy. This communion is a protection and privilege that you have in Me. Seek Me much.

I love you very much.

JANUARY 6

Daily Reading: 1 Kings 22:1-37

1 Cor. 14:33   *For God is not the author of confusion, but of peace, as in all churches of the saints.*

A great and mighty work is exploding on the scene. I am setting the captives free so they will be free to hear and obey Me. My sheep will know My voice.

A child must learn to recognize her father's voice. As he cares for and loves her, she will learn to respond to that love and listen for the father's voice.

Many people have been confused. There have been many voices speaking to them and they have not listened enough to My voice to know it. As a result they have assumed it was Me speaking to them, when actually it was their enemy. They are caught in traps and I want to free them.

I want to build relationships with them, as I had with Abraham and others, where they will trust Me and let Me guide them. I want to be their friend but a trust relationship must be established. The other voices will bring confusion, hurts and ultimately destroy them.

JANUARY 7

Daily Reading: 1 Thessalonians 5:14-23, Psalm 138

Ephesians 5:20   *Giving thanks always for all things unto God and the Father in the name of our Lord Jesus Christ;*

1 Thess. 5:18   *In everything give thanks: for this is the will of God in Christ Jesus concerning you.*

My child I am pleased with your praise. I rejoice in hearing your thanksgivings. A thankful heart is one that can grow in my faith. I want to minister My faith to you. Thankfulness will open that channel.

Rejoicing in Me will send the enemy packing. No discouragement can minister to you when you come to Me to rejoice in Me and thank Me for everything. My word declares "let all requests be made known in thanksgiving, and giving thanks for all things."

A joyous, thankful person will draw people. It creates a hunger in others for a similar experience. You are My light when you minister this, and the darkness will disappear when the light shines upon it. Do not retreat from the enemy; he too must back off when you radiate My light. He is afraid of exposure. He is fearful of My power and light in you. Light will always prevail over darkness.

JANUARY 8

Daily Reading: Joshua 10:12-14, Ecclesiastes 3:1-8

Eph. 5: 15-17 *See then that ye walk circumspectly, not as fools, but as wise, Redeeming the time, because the days are evil. Wherefore be ye not unwise, but understanding what the will of the Lord is.*

Go in my peace and do not allow Satan to make you think you have no time. The time spent with Me is the all-important thing.

The same principle applies to time as to tithing. When you give me of your time first, I will bless your efforts and give you more time.

I love you and I do not want to miss this time with you. My way is peace, but Satan's way is to bring you into a frenzy, to get you hurried and upset, and make you think there is no time.

Rest is also a state of mind. Your mind must be stayed on Me for I am your rest. I created time and you must rule it; it should not rule you. Let your mind be renewed and rejoice in Me. I have made this day.

JANUARY 9

Daily Reading: John 4:5-40

John 4:14 *But whosoever drinketh of the water that I shall give him shall never thirst; but the water that I shall give him shall be in him a well of water springing up into everlasting life.*

There is so much in My heart that I desire to share with you, My supply is endless. It is like a well with a spring in it, it will never run dry. It will always be cool and refreshing like that water on a hot and dry day. It will meet the need at that moment.

Daily you will need to hear from Me, the same as daily you need to drink from that well. You need water daily. When you are tired it will rejuvenate you and when you are down it will encourage you. Without water you will die and without Me speaking to your life, ministering to you, you will also die spiritually.

JANUARY 10

Daily Reading: Daniel 6

Daniel 6:10   *Now when Daniel knew that the writing was signed, he went into his house; and his windows being open in his chamber toward Jerusalem, he kneeled upon his knees three times a day, and prayed, and gave thanks before his God, as he did aforetime.*

My child you must seek Me daily. You can take the time, for the time spent with Me is the all-important time. Doing things and getting together with others is okay, but it is more important to spend time in My presence first.

I enjoy speaking to you this way and I miss you when you do not spend time with Me. I will guide and counsel you for each day as I love to fellowship with you! My presence is always there for you to lean on. Lean on Me. Let Me be your strength, your love, your life, your everything. Do not seek them from men, rather, seek them from Me. Then you too can be a Daniel and be victorious in any situation.

JANUARY 11

Daily Reading: Isaiah 55

Isaiah 55:8   *For My thoughts are not your thoughts, neither are your ways My ways, saith the Lord.*

My child, do not be surprised at My ways or My workings. My ways and workings are not your ways. Things may go differently than you think.

I love to surprise people as it shows them that I am God and that I am in control. Man can only see it from one way, but I can see it from all sides. My ways are not limited. I spoke this world into existence and at My word things will change and happen. Rest in Me. I desire to use you for My glory and I love you.

JANUARY 12

Daily Reading: Psalm 119:97-112

Romans 12:2   And be not conformed to this world: but be ye transformed by the renewing of your mind, that ye may prove what is that good, and acceptable, and perfect, will of God.

My ways supersede human ways and thinking. Seek My ways and directions continually. In this way you will not run ahead of Me. Let Me lead and guide you.

As you concentrate on Me, I will minister My peace to you. With My peace ruling in your heart and mind all turmoil must cease, and you will feel refreshed and able to go on.

Many things go through your mind but look to Me and let Me lead you. Most of the time it will not be at all the way your mind thought it would be. Your own thoughts can be deceiving. Your mind must be renewed in Me.

JANUARY 13

Daily Reading: Judges 6

Judges 6:12   And the angel of the Lord appeared unto him, and said unto him, The Lord is with thee, thou mighty man of valour.

Reclaim the land, take back territory that has been lost through unbelief. Press forward and be bold! This is going to become My territory and My land once again.

Many are in bondage but I have come to set the captives free. The powers of darkness are subject to My name. They can rule as long as they are given that right because of My people not taking their rightful place of authority and reclaiming the land.

I have given you the authority to rule over the spiritual world of darkness. I have crushed Satan under my feet and I desire for you to do the same. Many who are sick are that way because their soul cannot prosper. They have curses on their lives. They need to forgive and ask for forgiveness so that they can be set free. They must know the truth first and that will prepare the way for them to be set free.

JANUARY 14

Daily Reading: Psalm 61

Psalm 46:1   *God is our refuge and strength, a very present help in trouble.*

Let Me be your strong and mighty tower. In Me you will find safety and security. My children should always turn to Me. Let Me be your shield and your protector.

Principalities and powers would come against My work and seek to destroy it. They desire to come against My people, but you will have a safe refuge in Me. Flee to My presence into My safety.

I love you and I care for you. Your battle is not with people, therefore do not let your mind even dwell on them, but recognize who the enemy really is and know he has been and is defeated. I am your God, in Me the foe has been overcome and defeated.

JANUARY 15

Daily Reading: Genesis 18:16-33

Psalm 139: 17   *How precious also are thy thoughts unto me, O God! how great is the sum of them!*

I am pleased that you seek Me and acknowledge Me. Continue to do that more and more for I am always with you and there is so much I want to relate and share with you.

I desire close fellowship with My children. I desire for My children to share every aspect of their lives with Me. I want to have an important part.

When you love someone you desire to share everything with that person, your joys and your sorrows, your needs and your desires. You go to them first about anything that happens in your life because you care and you want them to share it with you. I love you and I desire to have that close a relationship with you.

JANUARY 16

Daily Reading: Isaiah 28

Isaiah 28:26   *For his God doth instruct him to discretion, and doth teach him.*

Keep looking to Me in all circumstances and I will build your faith. It grows here a little and there a little, line upon line, precept upon precept, one spoonful at a time. Keep your eyes on Me and delight to do My will and this will happen.

I am doing a work in this area of your faith and the gates of hell shall not prevail against it. Walk in My ways and My light and people will notice it. You will not draw attention, but the light will draw the attention.

I am pleased that you sought to take this time with Me. I will bless your day. I love you.

JANUARY 17

Daily Reading: John 10:25-30, Isaiah 26:1-8

Isaiah 26:3   *Thou wilt keep him in perfect peace, whose mind is stayed on Thee: because he trusteth in Thee.*

I am pleased that you cryout to Me when you are in distress. I love you. I will meet your needs and minister to you. I am your heavenly Father and you are My child and I desire to hold you close.

Do not let anything get in between us. When you give way to different thoughts expressing negatives, doubts, fears, condemnation, etc., it prevents Me from ministering to you. I do not leave you, but you have bound Me in that I cannot minister to you then.

I am at work here and in your life and I desire to give you My peace. When you feel weak physically or emotionally, ask Me to undergird you and commit yourself to Me. What has truly been committed to Me and placed in My hand,

no man can pluck out. You are safe with Me. I have you in the palm of My hand.
Go this day in My love and peace.

JANUARY 18

Daily Reading: Matthew 13:1-23

Mark 4:33-34   *And with many such parables spake the the word unto*
them, as they were able to hear it. But without a parable
spake He not unto them: and when they were alone, He
expounded all things to His disciples.

My words and thoughts are only hidden from those who do not seek Me for
them. My word is given to my body. If you seek Me, I will release an anointing
in your life to understand My Word.

There is nothing hidden that cannot be understood. I will make the way plain
to My sons and My daughters. Seek Me, for in Me are all the treasures of My
word.

JANUARY 19

Daily Reading: John 11:1-44

John 11:33,35   *When Jesus therefore saw her weeping, and the Jews also*
weeping which came with her, He groaned in the spirit,
and was troubled. Jesus wept.

I desire a close walk with My children, a trusting relationship. Let go and let
Me. When you hang on to preconceived ideas you cannot fully trust Me. I must
set the way and the means, you cannot, for then you would want Me to walk
the way you planned and that cannot be. You must follow Me, not the other
way around.

Remember I love you very much and I would never do anything to hurt you.
When you hurt, I hurt also. I feel the heartbeat of My children. In order to feel
their heartbeat I must be very close, and I am.

Nothing goes unnoticed; every sigh, every tear, every feeling, I am aware of
them all.

I will lead your day and bless you. All your strength and confidence is in Me.

JANUARY 20

Daily Reading: Galatians 4:1-7

John 12:24   *Verily, verily, I say unto you, Except a corn of wheat fall into the ground and die, it abideth alone: but if it die, it bringeth forth much fruit.*

I rejoice in what you have done. I accept what you laid on the altar for as you die to self, I can raise you up in the newness of My life.

It is My life and My anointing that will set you free, and will draw the needy. My life and My anointing is a light that shines and it will be seen by believers and unbelievers alike.

My son, My daughter, I love you and I am happy when I see growth taking place in you. I desire that truly you be a son, a daughter, and take up responsibilities for Me. I will bless you this day.

JANUARY 21

Daily Reading: Proverbs 2

Proverbs 2:6   *For the Lord giveth wisdom: out of His mouth cometh knowledge and understanding.*

Hebrews 12:28   *Wherefore we receiving a kingdom which cannot be moved, let us have grace, whereby we may serve God acceptably with reverence and godly fear:*

I am all wisdom and knowledge. The more you enter into what I have for you, the more there will yet be to discover and experience.

You are where I want you to be at this time. There is a shaking going on, but that which is of Me will remain. Do not fear but trust Me. Winds may blow, storms may rage, but keep your eyes and heart rooted in Me and you won't be moved. Only the chaff blows away.

Rejoice in Me. I love you and I am pleased when you seek Me more and more.

JANUARY 22

Daily Reading: Jeremiah 1:11-19

Lam. 3:22,23   *It is of the Lord's mercies that we are not consumed, because His compassions fail not. They are new every morning: great is Thy faithfulness.*

You are My child and I delight to bless you. Spend this day proclaiming My goodness. There will never fail to come to pass any of the promises that I have made to you.

My children know what is going on; the world does not! You can have peace in your heart, because you know I am in control. You will have assurance where others have turmoil. My confidence will be your portion.

I will also protect My servants and those that do what I command them to do. Draw close to Me and I will draw close to you. There will be things happening that you will not understand, but remember I love you and I care for you, and all things are in My control.

JANUARY 23

Daily Reading: Matthew 15:1-20

Isaiah 29:13   *Wherefore the Lord said, Forasmuch as this people draw near Me with their mouth, and with their lips do honour Me, but have removed their heart far from Me, and their fear toward Me is taught by the precept of men:*

I desire pure and holy hearts filled with My mercy and truth. When your heart is right before Me then there is no doublemindedness in your life. Sometimes it becomes easy to act and to be a certain way, but your heart is not in it. That is not right.

I desire a pure vessel; pure in heart, soul and mind. These three must be one. They must appear outwardly the same as they are inwardly. There can be no double standards in My kingdom. I look at the heart and I judge heart motives.

I will be with you this day and bless you.

JANUARY 24

Daily Reading: Hebrews 11:32-40 12:1-4

Hebrews 12:1   *Wherefore seeing we also are compassed about with so great a cloud of witnesses, let us lay aside every weight, and the sin which doth so easily beset us, and let us run with patience the race that is set before us,*

Things may be happening that you do not understand but by keeping your eyes on Me they will not throw you off track.

You are running a race and you must keep your eyes on the finish line, which is the goal that I have set before you. Things will come that will seem like hindrances or obstacles, but keep going by looking to Me, the author and finisher of your faith.

Some hurdles are meant to be jumped over, others you will go around. Keep your eyes on Me and you will finish the race and be a winner. Satan would put these hindrances in your way but do not dwell on them. As you pass over each hurdle, you defeat his purpose, which is to stop you from looking to Me.

You will be a winner for I am a winner. I have not lost once. I am victorious and you can be too!!

JANUARY 25

Daily Reading: Deuteronomy 5:6-11 Psalm 119:10-16

Matthew 22:37   *Jesus said unto him, Thou shalt love the Lord thy God with all thy heart, and with all thy soul, and with all thy mind.*

Let My word dwell in you richly. There is much that you do not understand. Let Me minister My word through you. Be a living epistle for me.

I must have first place in your heart. Do not let other things take that place. Guard My place in your heart. Those other things cannot help you. They cannot minister to your needs. They will minister, but it will draw you away from Me.

I love you, but I am a jealous lover for I desire to be first. All other things and activities must come under My control.

JANUARY 26

Daily Reading: James 2:14-26

James 1:22   *But be ye doers of the word, and not hearers only, deceiving your own selves.*

My child you need discipline, self discipline. Your mind quickly sees what you should or shouldn't do, but you hesitate many times to carry it out. The same principle is in My word, "Faith without works is dead", so it is in your life. You can think about all kinds of things, but it is to no avail unless it is carried out. You must make your body do it. You are in control of your body only when you do those things that need doing.

Call on Me to be your help and guide. Sitting there thinking about it will not get it done. Ask Me to change you and then be obedient to My promptings. With Me and in Me you can do all things.

JANUARY 27

Daily Reading: Matthew 10:24-42

2 Timothy 2:3   *Thou therefore endure hardness, as a good soldier of Jesus Christ.*

The enemy does not want my army to fight and disarm him. Man cannot hurt you, but My word declares, "I have the power to hurt and to heal." Satan must bow under My power. Man can be used as a tool in the hand of Satan, but in My hands you can be a greater tool.

In an army situation, a soldier must obey orders. He is not asked how he feels about it. He trusts his commander and chief and I ask you to trust Me, but there is a difference. I love you and I care for you, I gave My life for you. All other is counterfeit, it only satisfies for the moment.

I will bring lasting peace and joy and contentment. Go in My peace and joy and contentment this day.

JANUARY 28

Daily Reading: Proverbs 29

Revelation 3:19   As many as I love, I rebuke and chasten: be zealous therefore, and repent.

Yes My child, I am doing agood work in you. The pruning may hurt but the fruit will be great. I have let you be the way you've acted and spoken lately, so you could see for yourself how bad your attitude really is.

I desire to set you totally free, but you must hate and fall into disagreement with, those attitudes. Purpose in your heart to let Me speak through you. Give your rights to Me.

I love you so much. I died for you. I sacrificed Myblood for you. I care very much for you. You are precious and you are beloved.

JANUARY 29

Daily Reading: 2 Kings 18:1-8; 19:10-20,35-37

Proverbs 22:19   That thy trust may be in the Lord, I have made known to thee this day, even to thee.

I am leading you My son and My daughter. My way may not have been your way or even the way you would have chosen but I can see the end from the beginning and I know My way is best.

I am pleased that you trust Me and that you express that trust in Me. That gives Me the authority to take your hand and gently lead you. My hand is so much bigger than yours and you can rest and feel comforted in Me.

I love you both. Rejoice in Me and praise Me much for l am doing a good thing. My ways are higher than your ways.

JANUARY 30

Daily Reading: Mark 8:22-38

Mark 7:17   *And when He was entered into the house front the people, His disciples asked Him concerning the parable.*

I love you; you are My friend. I am pleased that you seek this time to spend with Me. There is so much that I have and that I desire to speak to My friends and My body. So many do not realize that I will speak to them personally.

When I walked this earth, I had intimate conversations with My disciples and that hasn't stopped. I still desire intimate conversations with My disciples; those that are close to Me; those that walk with Me every day. They are never far from Me; they were always with Me. They witnessed the miracles that I did. They ate with Me and slept with Me, we had everything in common.

This day is a gift from Me. Rejoice and be glad in it! I will go with you this day.

JANUARY 31

Daily Reading: John 13

John 13:34,35   *A new commandment I give unto you, That ye love one another; as I have loved you, that ye also love one another. By this shall all men know that ye are My disciples, if ye have love one to another.*

How I love you; you are My beloved. I wish that My children would realize how much I love them. I know all your innermost desires. I know you better than you know yourself. I desire to let you know more of Me and My workings and to know yourself better. I desire to use you completely.

Yield all of yourself to Me for what you hold back will often ensnare you and cause you grief and hurt. I can take better care of you than you can yourself. Man thinks he must first look out for himself and then for others. I say abandon yourself to Me and I will show you how to look out for others and I will look after you.

Do not withdraw into yourself to hide, but hide in Me for I will be your shield and your protector.

FEBRUARY 1

Daily Reading: Proverbs 26:17-28

1 Thess. 4:11   *And that ye study to be quiet, and to do your own business, and to work with your own hands, as we commanded you;*

I love you and I am happy to unfold My plan for your life. You have sensed right, I look on the heart and not on outward appearances. Keep your heart pure, do not backslide in your heart. Do not look to others unless they look to Me only, for all that they do is in vain.

You concern yourself with many things that are not in your control. You need only to seek Me. Hide yourself in Me and be obedient to what I command you. Many concerns can become burdens, that were not meant to be yours.

Rejoice in Me this day.

FEBRUARY 2

Daily Reading: 1 Samuel 17:32-37; Matthew 18:11-14

John 10:14   *I am the good shepherd, and know My sheep, and am known of Mine.*

I will lead you and guide you because you are Mine. I am your shepherd and I watch out for My flock. I desire for you to stay close to Me and you will as long as your eyes are fixed on Me. When you focus on other thoughts and words you lose sight of Me, so remain focused on Me.

Wherever I am there is safety and protection and My love. No wild enemy will come to the shepherd, but they will attack the sheep that have wandered away and are defenseless. Do not wander off but stay close by My side. Feed on My words.

FEBRUARY 3

Daily Reading: 2 Samuel 22

2 Samuel 22:29   For Thou an my lamp, 0 Lord: and the Lord will lighten my darkness.

v:47   The Lord liveth; and blessed be my rock; and exalted be the God of the rock of my salvation.

You are beautiful when you show forth My joy and peace. I am in control of your life and I move and rule situations as I please, to bring glory and praise and honour to Me. Rejoice in Me, stand and see the salvation of your God. Do not give up or give way to discouragement. My ways are much greater.

Believe Me and continue to encourage others. Let My light shine for My light will dispel the dark just like the morning will chase the dark night away. It has been ordained so. With the morning light comes the promise of a new day. My peace comes before the activities of the day set in.

Look to Me the author and finisher of your faith; who for the glory set before Him endured the cross and the shame. My glory is set before you, enter in and be partakers of Me. Have a blessed day, I love you.

FEBRUARY 4

Daily Reading: Exodus 19

Hebrews 10:22   Let us draw near with a true heart in full assurance of faith, having our hearts sprinkled from an evil conscience, and our bodies washed with pure water.

This day is ordained of Me. I have made this day for my people. Lift your voice up to Me today. All of creation must worship Me.

I am God, pure and holy is My name. All that is not pure and holy cannot abide in My presence.

I desire to take off the bands of bondages that rob My people from entering fully into My presence. I came for that reason, to set My people free from the bondages of sin and allow them to enter into My presence. Because I am pure and holy those areas of bondages and sin must be removed before My people can fully enter in to Me.

Rejoice in Me this day and worship Me with all your being. I rejoice in the worship of My people!

FEBRUARY 5
Daily Reading: Exodus 13:17-22; Deuteronomy 8

Luke 12:28,29   *If then God so clothe the grass, which is today in the field, and tomorrow is cast into the oven; how much more will he clothe you, o ye of little faith? And seek not ye what ye shall eat, or what ye shall drink, neither be ye of doubtful mind.*

I am your heavenly Father. I love you and I take care of you. No one can hurt a hair on your head without My permission. Rejoice in that!

You are always surrounded by My protection. When you doubt that, you open yourself up for attack from the enemy. It does not depend on feeling; it is a fact, a sure knowledge from Me.

The cloud protected the Israelites in the desert. It was not just a cloud; it was My presence, to keep them and watch over them. I provided for them and I desire to do the same for you.

Bless Me and I will bless you. Whatsoever you do unto others, that will also be done unto you. Rest in My love. I desire to be your protector, guide, friend, father, etc. I want to be everything to you. I love you.

FEBRUARY 6

Daily Reading: Ephesians 6:10-18; Joshua 5:13-15

Joshua 1:9   *Have not I commanded thee? Be strong and of a good courage; be not afraid, neither be thou dismayed: for the Lord thy God is with thee whithersoever thou goest.*

Proclaim My truth! Be bold! Do not let the enemy discourage you, but press on. The kingdom of heaven cometh by violence and the violent taketh by force.

No war can be won just by talking about it, but by actually fighting the enemy it can be won. So get out and fight. I am your captain and I will lead you into battle. Prepare, put on your armour and gird your weapons. Be ready; the battle lines are forming.

Remember I have promised you the victory!

FEBRUARY 7

Daily Reading: Matthew 10:5-16; Luke 10:17-20

Matthew 16:19   *And I will give unto thee the keys of the kingdom of heaven: and whatsoever thou shalt bind on earth shall be bound in heaven: and whatsoever thou shalt loose on earth shall be loosed in heaven.*

My children, I love you. You are under My control. All situations are under My control. I never lose control. I have won the battle and the victory is Mine. It is completed. My people you must realize this and take hold of it.

Every enemy within you has been defeated and when you speak in My name and authority, he must leave. He can live there no longer. I desire to see My people set free.

I desire for My people to enter into all the blessings that I have for you. I do not like to see you robbed of your blessings. The demonic force would like to steal those blessings from you, but do not allow it and do not let him intimidate you. He has to let go at My word.

FEBRUARY 8

Daily Reading: Psalm 3

Psalm 3:3 *But thou, O Lord, art a shield for me; my glory, and the lifter up of mine head.*

I love you. I love all of My creation. I have created everything. I sent My son to redeem man and to break the curse of sin. I rejoice when man in return loves and praises Me.

Do not be discouraged at the attacks that are coming your way. I am the lifter up of your head. I will set you up on high. I have called you and I am doing a good thing in your life. My way is not always a smooth highway. However, it does not stop at a barrier, but it will continue on. I prepare the way and I will lead and guide you. Be of good cheer; I love you.

FEBRUARY 9

Daily Reading: Psalm 16

Colossians 3:15 *And let the peace of God rule in your hearts, to the which also ye are called in one body; and be ye thankful.*

Praise Me for everything. There is not a hair on your head that can fall off without Me knowing about it.

I see your inner turmoil. You are not resting in Me. When everything is not under my control there is turmoil. When you are in control the result is also turmoil. You are allowing Satan to rule your mind, will and emotions. My will must become your will, My thoughts must become your thoughts and My life must become your life.

I love you and I desire the best for you. Give of yourself to Me and be obedient to Me. Trust Me completely and rejoice in Me this day!

FEBRUARY 10
Daily Reading: Hebrews 12:5-24

> *Proverbs 3:11,12   My son, despise not the chastening of the Lord; neither be weary of His correction: For whom the Lord loveth He correcteth; even as a father the son in whom he delighteth.*

Do not fear My dealings and do not run away from Me. In Me there is safety. I will not allow one hair to fall off your head without My permission. You belong to Me and I have your best interest at heart.

I love you and I do not desire to chastise you, but to point out My way and to have you walk in it obediently. You will be enlarged and stretched, but by remaining close to Me you will not be as aware of the dealings.

I desire to use you more and fill you more with My Holy Spirit. My ways will not be your ways, so don't try to figure it out. Just love Me and stay close to Me.

Rejoice in Me and let Me rejoice in you.

FEBRUARY 11
Daily Reading: Matthew 7:24-27, Genesis 9:9-17.

> *Genesis 9:11   And I will establish My covenant with you; neither shall all flesh be cut off any more by the waters of a flood; neither shall there any more be a flood to destroy the earth.*

I am building a firm foundation in your life. Storms may come and storms may go, but the house that is built upon the rock will stand. Your house has been built on Me the Rock. When the storms come and rage all around you, you will have My peace.

I am your foundation; not your feelings, not people, not situations. The storms and rains cannot move or hurt a solid foundation. The waves will hit it and maybe even wash over it, but it will remain firm, strong and solid, and those waves will have lost their thrust. The rains will come, but they will stop again.

I have promised never again to completely flood the world. So it is in your life; the rains of situations may come upon you, but when you look to My promise, the rainbow, they can notcome high enough to drown you. I am your solid foundation that will not crumble.

I love you. Have a safe day; I am watching over you.

FEBRUARY 12
Daily reading: 2 Samuel 11

Job 31:1   *I made a covenant with my eyes; why then should I think upon a maid?*

Let Me cleanse your heart and your mind. You must walk in the truths that I have given you. Just knowing them isn't good enough, but start disciplining yourself not even to give those things that would defile you a second glance.

My word is pure and holy. I am pure and holy. Much that is unholy and impure starts by what you see and then it consumes your thought life. It needs to be confessed, forgiven and cleansed and your mind renewed by My Spirit.

FEBRUARY 13
Daily Reading: Ephesians 1:15-23

Philippians 3:10 That I may know Him, and the power of His resurrection, and the fellowship of His sufferings, being made conformable unto His death;

My greatness is something you cannot comprehend. Your finite mind cannot understand the infinite God. I am Lord of all.

I know My people and I desire that they know Me. I know every hair on their heads, and the very heartbeat that is within their body. Your mind cannot comprehend how well I know My children. I love them, but I desire that they get to know Me better.

I am pleased that you seek this time with Me. You are getting to know Me better because of it. Keep your heart tuned to Mine this day.

FEBRUARY 14
Daily Reading: Luke 10:29-37

1 Peter 3:8   *Finally, be ye all of one mind, having compassion one of*
                    another, love as brethren, be pitiful, be courteous:

Ephesians 5:29   *For no man ever yet hated his own flesh; but nourisheth*
                    and cherisheth it, even as the Lord the church:

You can't imagine the depth of feeling I have for My people, the joy I experience or the hurt I feel. I want to give you My feelings and My heartbeat, so that you will be able to respond to My body's needs the way I do. You will know and say, "Jesus is feeling this or that for you, and you will feel it too." My compassion touches and changes lives. Your compassion must totally become My compassion.

I love you and the rest of My body very much. I do not love in measure according to how they respond to Me, I love because I am love. Once they have been grafted into My body, I see them only as My body. If a man does not love his own body he cannot love anyone else. Loving is accepting. I the Lord will change the person, but I accept them.

FEBRUARY 15
Daily Reading: John 16:16-33

John 16:33   *These things I have spoken unto you, that in Me ye might*
                    have peace. In the world ye shall have tribulation: but be
                    of good cheer; I have overcome the world.

My child, I love you. Why do you let the enemy rob you of your joy and peace. My peace I give to you, turn to Me; I am peace. My child rest assured I am in control; I have not left you or forsaken you. Shortly you will see My plan unfold.

There are good things in store for you. Training does not go on forever. I am doing a good thing in your life. You are hid in Me and I will reassure you when you need it.

Rejoice and sing before me My child. Live one day at a time for My peace is here for you.

FEBRUARY 16

Daily Reading: Genesis 27:41-44,33:1-16

Proverbs 29:25   *The fear of man bringeth a snare: but whoso putteth his trust in the Lord shall be safe.*

Yes, I will complete the healing in the relationship with your loved ones. Do not always expect them to understand everything you say or do. Sometimes the understanding is for you only. Love them and share with them the things I have done in your life.

Do not attack things that they hold dear or are in bondage to, but with love and understanding speak to them. Anything spoken that is not motivated by My love and understanding will cause them to quickly put up defensive walls. Never fear confrontations but use them as opportunities to minister my love.

Enjoy My presence this day!

FEBRUARY 17

Daily Reading: Psalm 17

Psalm 17:8   *Keep me as the apple of the eye, hide me under the shadow of thy wings.*

John 21:20a.   *Then Peter, turning about, seeth the disciple WhomJesus loved following; which also leaned on His breast at supper.*

My child, I love you very much. My arms are around you. When you are being hugged it is an indication of love and it is not meant for hurt. My arms are around you so rest in Me.

Do not do anything, but lean your head, including all your thoughts, on Me. Let Me minister My peace and rest to you. Storms may come, but when you are leaning against Me you are sheltered from those storms.

Snuggle, don't struggle. Enjoy My presence, enjoy My love, enjoy Me.

FEBRUARY 18
Daily Reading: Exodus 15:22-27; 1John 1:5-10

1 John 1:5,6   This then is the message which we have heard of Him, and declare unto you, that God is light, and in Him is no darkness at all. If we say that we have fellowship with Him, and walk in darkness, we lie, and do not the truth:

My son, My daughter, I love you. Rest in Me this day. Rejoice in Me. Seek Me in everything and seek Me continually. Even when things seemingly all go against you, remember I am still watching over you.

I will use every situation for the furtherance of My kingdom. Satan's plan is for harm, but My plan is for good. A victory has been won if it brings you closer to Me.

I desire to impart My wisdom and knowledge in every situation. My way is light and in Me is no darkness. Darkness cannot comprehend things, but in the light all things are made clear. Understand My love for you.

FEBRUARY 19

Daily Reading: Nehemiah 6

Nehemiah 6:13   Therefore was he hired, that I should be afraid, and do so, and sin, and that they might have matter for an evil report, that they might reproach me.

I will lead and guide you this day. What Satan intends for evil, I will turn into a blessing. You have sensed right; you still have fears in your life and fear causes torment. Bring your fears to Me, confess them as sin and rebuke them.

You are fighting a good warfare and are making headway in Satan's territory causing him to lose and move backwards. He is angry and so more reinforcements have been coming against both of you.

Rely on Me, praise Me for the good work I am doing. I am victorious. Cover yourself with My blood this day. Arm yourself with My armour.

I love you both, as you endure these hardships you are becoming better soldiers.

FEBRUARY 20

Daily Reading: Matthew 25:31-46

Matthew 25:40   And the King shall answer and say unto them, Verily I say unto you, Inasmuch as ye have done it unto one of the least of these My brethren, ye have done it unto Me.

Whatever is done with a pure heart to Me, will be recognized as being Me in you. I desire to come forth full in you.

Sometimes you do things because you want approval of man. That is not necessarily bad, but your motive must be to want approval from Me. Your heart must be one of love and adoration for Me. Out of that love whatever you do will be pleasing to Me. When you seek praise from Me, you will have your reward.

Love others as you would want to be loved. Serve others as you would desire to be served. Pray for others as you would desire to be prayed for.

FEBRUARY 21

Daily Reading: Matthew 26:69-75, John 21:15-19

Luke 15:21,22   And the son said unto him, Father, I have sinned against heaven, and in thy sight, and am no more worthy to be called thy son. But the father said to his servants, Bring forth the best robe, and put it on him; and put a ring on his hand, and shoes on his feet:

I love all My children equally. Some of them are more aware of this love than others, but I desire for all My children to be aware of My love for them. I do not minister rejection so if they feel rejection, it does not come from Me.

No negative emotion comes from Me. My people you need discernment and teaching and wisdom. Bring every negative emotion to Me, hand it over completely. I desire to heal and mend the broken hearted. I am a restorer of breaches.

FEBRUARY 22

Daily Reading: Acts 4:13-31

Psalm 16:11   *Thou wilt shew me the path of life: in Thy presence is fulness of joy; at thy right hand there are pleasures for evermore.*

My child, I love you. Remain in My presence all the time. Remain sensitive to Me. Do not look to others and do not judge or criticize them. Keep your eyes focused only on Me. When you see only Me in all situations, then you are reflecting Me.

Do not give way to becoming tired of the road that is before you but keep your eyes steadfastly on Me. I have a good plan for your life. More and more you are reflecting Me; My wisdom, My joy, My peace, My knowledge, My patience and My love.

The more you are in My presence the more you will be like Me. Be in My presence this day as you do your work. In My presence there is fulness of joy.

FEBRUARY 23

Daily Reading: Psalm 41

Psalm 41:9   *Yea, mine own familiar friend, in whom I trusted, which did eat of my bread, hath lifted up his head against me.*

Learn to rest in Me in all things. I am in control over every situation. Hurts may spring upin your life that you have no control over, but remember I do. Nothing comes your way without Me knowing about it. Do not fear the hurts, but let Me bring a healing and restoration to the situation. It will be better than before because I Will perform surgery and take out that which is rotten and stinks and causes pain. I will bring healing to your body.

Rest in Me and let Me bring the healing. You have been hurt, but I will heal you, for I love you My child.

FEBRUARY 24
Daily Reading: Matthew 26:31-35,47-56

Proverbs 16:32   *He that is slow to anger is better than the mighty; and he that ruleth his spirit than he that taketh a city.*

My child, I love you. I will be with you this day. There are things in your life that still need to be brought into a balance. You must learn not to let your feelings rule you for it is your will that should be in control. A will totally yielded to Me.

When the enemy knows that you obey every emotion that you feel, he will attack you in those areas. For instance, if thoughts of anger or frustration can immobilize you, he will try to provoke you to anger. Whatever rules you at times, whether it is feelings, desires, emotions or appetites, must be placed under My control.

FEBRUARY 25
Daily Reading: Daniel 4:28-37

Psalm 12:3   *The Lord shall cut off all flattering lips, and the tongue that speaketh proud things:*

I desire to set you free from your hurts and insecurities. Seek My approval more than you seek man's approval. Sometimes you have that reversed.

I see that you want to put to death that proud, know-it-all spirit. It must be replaced with My humility and thankfulness. Have a thankful heart because I have given you the ability to learn and remember what you have been taught.

Bless and thank Me this day for everything that has come your way.

FEBRUARY 26
Daily Reading: Acts 8:3-8, 26-40

Acts 8:5,8   *Then Philip went down to the city of Samaria, and preached Christ unto them. And there was great joy in that city.*

See how the snow is falling, oh so gently down! That is how My Spirit works. It moves and works steadily and continually, but oh so gently. You cannot hear it and you may not be aware of it, but you will see the results for My Spirit is always at work.

A revival has started in this land and in this city. My Spirit is at work. You may not see it or hear it, but just as the snow comes gently down, in a matter of time, you will surely see it. Those who know Me intimately will see it and will rejoice and will give Me thanks for it. They will desire to be a part in it. Rejoice in Me this day!

FEBRUARY 27
Daily Reading: Numbers 13:17-33

Numbers 13:30   *And Caleb stilled the people before Moses, and said, Let us go up at once, and possess it; for we are well able to overcome it.*

My child, I love you! You are precious to Me. Rejoice in Me this day. You have become an overcomer in Me. You will have a vital part in My kingdom. Praise Me for that!

Let your light shine for Me this day. Be faithful in whatever I ask of you.

Your roots have gone down deep and you know how to tap into Me for all your resources. Never fail to do this. Your strength is not in self, but in Me. You will need Me constantly for I take your burdens and ease your loads. My strength will carry them and see you through. In Me there is victory!

FEBRUARY 28

Daily Reading: Genesis 37

Proverbs 20:24   *Man's goings are of the Lord; how can a man then understand his own way?*

You are in My perfect will. I will go before you every step of the way. Keep your heart pure before Me. Love Me and love My body, whether they understand or not. Thank Me for all I have taught you and ministered to you in the past, but My training will not stop there. I will continue to show and reveal more of Myself and My plan to you as you yield yourself completely to Me.

I love you and My protection is around you at this time. I see your tears. You have been hurt and you have felt hurt and rejection coming your way. Be assured that it is not coming from Me. I am your balm in Gilead. I understand the complete situation. Above all you are precious to Me.

MARCH 1

Daily Reading: Numbers 12

Numbers 12:3   *(Now the man Moses was very meek, above all the men which were upon the face of the earth.)*

Matthew 11:29 *Take My yoke upon you, and learn of Me; for I am meek and lowly in heart: and ye shall find rest unto your souls.*

My child, meekness is of Me. It is preferring the other person in love before yourself. Meekness means gentleness, humbling yourself and putting down pride of self. It also means removing yourself out of the way and letting My power and authority move through you. Allowing nothing of yourself to rise up and take the glory.

Yes, meekness is a fruit of the Spirit and it grows in you. It grows bigger as it remains fastened to the tree and gets its food from the roots. The tree will also receive special treatment such as, pruning, insecticide to kill bugs and insects, fertilizer, water and sunshine, enabling it to grow. I, the farmer and husbandman, do all these things to the tree so it will bear good fruit and I will be pleased.

MARCH 2

Daily Reading: Exodus 3

Proverbs 4:20-22 *My Son, attend to my words: incline thine ear unto my sayings. Let them not depart from thine eyes; keep them in the midst of thine heart. For they are life unto those that find them, and health to all their flesh.*

You need My word to refresh you, encourage you and to give direction to your life. My word is wisdom, knowledge, truth, healing, restoration and it overcomes. My word is Me. What I say, I am. I have not changed.

Moses needed to know who I was. I was, I am, and I am to come. I have not changed. I led Moses step by step and I will lead you step by step.

I will go before you and I am behind you. I will give light and protection. No matter how dark the dark seems, My pillar of light is always there to dispel the darkness. There will come dark times, but do not try to look into the darkness, instead look up at the light overhead.

MARCH 3

Daily Reading: 2 Kings 4:1-7,38-44

I Peter 5:7,8   *Casting all your care upon Him; for He careth for you. Be sober, be vigilant; because your adversary the devil, as a roaring lion, walketh about, seeking whom, he may devour:*

My child, you are doing well in bringing small details to Me. They are the ones I want to have a part in. Many times the big situations that you have no problem with, you bring to Me, but I also want to have a part in the small minute details.

I rejoice in being able to help in all situations, the small and large. Ask Me to help you in your work. When I am leading you, you can get many things accomplished without feeling agitated, frustrated or anxious for those feelings are not from Me.

Rejoice in Me; I am beside you every moment of this day.

MARCH 4

Daily Reading: Exodus 23:20-33

Exodus 23:20   *Behold, I send an Angel before thee, to keep thee in the way, and to bring thee into the place which I have prepared.*

I am the answer to all your needs. More and more that knowledge has to be fixed in your heart so you will become unmovable when things come your way. Feelings change, but I do not change.

I love you. You desire the best for those you love and I desire the same for you. Bind every force that would come against you and ask Me for angelic protection. You must ask and then I will answer.

Rejoice in Me! I will be with you this day and My love will surround you. My presence will go with you this day.

MARCH 5

Daily Reading: 1 Corinthians 2:6-16

Luke 16:13a.   *No servant can serve two masters: for either he will hate the one, and love the other; or else he will hold to the one, and despise the other.*

When you live in My kingdom your citizenship is no longer this earth. You cannot serve two masters, yet many of My people try to do exactly that. My ways and rules are not accepted in this world for the world hates Me.

The ruler of this world is Satan and he is constantly challenging My people. Obey Me, seek Me, love Me, and I will be your guide and your king. Satan is constantly changing his rules and ways and disguising them. He will say it is a new thing, so Christians will obey him, stumble and fall.

Whatever your eyes are fastened upon there your heart will follow. I desire a pure heart and total allegiance and in return I will minister to you My joy and peace.

MARCH 6

Daily Reading: Romans 8:16-23

Genesis 1:26   *And God said, Let Us make man in Our image, after Our likeness: and let them have dominion over the fish of the sea, and over the fowl of the air, and over the cattle, and over all the earth, and over every creeping thing that creepeth upon the earth.*

My creation, the plants, animals and the elements are waiting for My children to take their place of authority and to speak to them. If Satan chooses to use them in any way, they must obey. Only the authority of a believer speaking in My name can set them free.

Seek My wisdom and revelation to know My will and then speak it into the situation. My creation seeks to glorify Me, their God. So ask Me for much wisdom, and I will grant it to you.

MARCH 7

Daily Reading: Ephesians 5:1-12

John 1:47   *Jesus saw Nathanael coming to Him, and saith of him, Behold an Israelite indeed, in whom is no guile!*

When you confess your sins, I am faithful and just to forgive you your sins and to cleanse you from all unrighteousness. Speak only truth and let no shades of other meanings come through. I must have no guile. Aim to please Me and in so doing, you will be pleasing to others.

I will bless your day as I blessed Nathanael's day. I love you.

MARCH 8
Daily Reading: Matthew 18:1-10

Psalm 119:165   *Great peace have they which love Thy law: and nothing*
shall offend them.

Do not take up offenses for other people. People want to be needed and so
Satan will use this need and try to fill it by taking up offences. Man's pride and
ego also gets fed in the process. It makes him feel important to get drawn into
a situation where he thinks his advise is needed.

I do use people to minister to others but in most situations you turn to Me as
a last resort for all wisdom and all knowledge In doing so you must humble
yourself and acknowledge that you know nothing and that you cannot do
anything except to let Me handle it. Often man will turn to man and the bad
feelings and attitudes that are ministering will be passed on to whomever you
are sharing with. What you really want to hear is that you're right and the other
person is wrong. You do not want to listen to true counsel which might lead to
forgiveness and cleansing.

Always keep Me before you and let My word lead and guide you. When your
eyes are on Me, you will not be offended.

MARCH 9
Daily Reading: Matthew 26:36-46

John 4:34   *Jesus saith unto them, My meat is to do the will of Him*
that sent Me, and to finish His work.

John 6:38   *For I came down from heaven, not to do Mine own will,*
but the will of Him that sent Me.

Seek My face continually. In Me is everything for I am all things. I love you and
I desire to fill you and use you. Seek My will in every situation for when you
know My will, you will do exactly what I would have you to do.

Love those who do not love you. Bless them and curse them not. What you bind
on earth is bound in heaven. Loosen My power to work in difficult situations.

Do not hang on to things yourself but place every situation in My hand. When it is released to Me I can act in the situation. Walk in My peace this day.

MARCH 10

Daily Reading: Ephesians 4:1-16

Joe 12:11a.   *And the Lord shall utter His voice before His army: for His camp is very great: for He is strong that executeth His word:*

You are being enlisted in My army and the marching orders are coming. In an army there is no individuality. You are part of that greater body called the army. There are different levels, but the office will stand out, not the person. Depending on what rank and office you hold, will show to others the amount of authority you have. Individuality is also lost in the fact that you all dress in uniform, making each one the same as the next.

In your personal relationship with Me you will always be an individual. There you can be My son or My daughter for no matter what the age or position a person has, to the parents he remains their child. I am your heavenly Father and I desire a close relationship with My children.

MARCH 11

Daily Reading: Acts 3

Galatians 6:10   *As we have therefore opportunity, let us do good unto all men, especially unto them who are of the household of faith.*

My son and My daughter, My hand is upon your life. You are both in My care and I am directing your paths. I will lead you both this day, Marvelous things are unfolding. When you abide in Me, My life will flow through you to others. I can use your life to liberate others.

Encourage those you meet this day. I will lead them to you so let them know that they count in My eyes. As you do this My body will grow and you will all feel part of one body and part of Me. I love you both and I desire to be in control this day.

MARCH 12

Daily Reading: Mark 9:1-29

Mark 9:2   *And after six days Jesus taketh with him Peter, and James, and John, and leadeth them, up into an high mountain apart by themselves: and He was transfigured before them.*

Yes My child, it is great to climb to the top of the mountain. Things take on a different perspective there. You can look back and see the valley below you and all the roads down there, but there is only one way to the top. You must push forward. You cannot rush or you will get out of breath. Take small steps, continually climbing higher and you will reach the top. It is exhilarating! You will notice that the temperature is much colder and the air is thinner and that not much grows up there. You will also notice that you are far away from the people for they are all in the valley where there is an abundance of growth.

Your mountain top experiences will excite you but will not help you to relate to people. To do that you must be in the valley where the people and the problems are. You must intermingle with them to relate with them. Only those who have climbed that mountain with you can also experience that high with you.

MARCH 13

Daily Reading: John 17

John 17:23   *I in them, and Thou in Me, that they may be made perfect in one; and that the world may know that thou hast sent Me, and hast loved them, as Thou hast loved Me.*

I am happy that you desire fellowship with Me. I want to be first in your life.

I have given you this day, go in My presence. My presence is here with you and I am with your loved ones back home also. I am an omnipresent God.

I am a personal God for each individual child. I love My children equally. I desire for My children to be close to Me. We must be a close knit family so that the world may see that we love one another. Love all of My people and when you find this difficult, ask Me to help you to see them as I see them.

MARCH 14

Daily Reading: Psalm 32

Psalm 32:5   *I acknowledged my sin unto thee, and mine iniquity have I not hid. I said, I will confess my transgressions unto the Lord; and Thou forgavest the iniquity of my sin.*

I am a God of mercy. When you confess your sins before Me, I will forgive them and remember them no more. Without My mercy and grace no one could stand before Me. I will pardon iniquity to those who humbly seek Me for it. I died for those sins and My death was not in vain.

I love my people and desire to set them free from every bondage of sin. I have gone ahead of you and I have won the victory over Satan. Walk in My victory and My word will not return void.

MARCH 15

Daily Reading: Hebrews 4:1-11

Hebrews 4:10   *For he that is entered into his rest, he also hath ceased from his own works, as God did from his.*

Rest in Me for there is nothing that frustrates the enemy more than you having rest in Me. Rest speaks of a trust and reliance on Me, and a peace in your heart. Rest in Me and all anxiety and fear will go.

My will is being accomplished in your life. Do not worry about what other people will say or think, just remember your life is hid in Me and it is Me that is being attacked not you.

Anxieties and fears are a ploy and a snare that the enemy will use to rob you of rest and peace, which I desire to give you. I love you. Rest in Me.

MARCH 16

Daily Reading: Jeremiah 1:1-10

Jeremiah 1:5   *Before I formed thee in the belly I knew thee; and before thou camest forth out of the womb I sanctified thee, and I ordained thee a prophet unto the nations.*

Lay aside all doubts and fears for they are not of Me. You are in My keeping power and I am able to keep you. I am with you and I will be with you. I am at work on your behalf.

Express confidence in Me for I am your anchor, it is not people's opinions or what people can or cannot see. Your life is hid in Me. I am happy that you want to spend time with Me this day. I am in control of your life. Welcome that control in your life. Sit back and let Me unfold the plan for your life. I love you!

MARCH 17

Daily Reading: 2 Chronicles 7

2 Chronicles 7:15 Now mine eyes shall be open, and my ears attent
unto the prayer that is made in this place.

Yes I care very much. Do not doubt My love for you. I have invested My life in you.

I am a good listener and My ears are always open to the cries and prayers of My people. I delight in the prayers of My people. In Me are all your answers so continue to bring your needs and desires before Me. Do not try to figure out what I am doing for I am doing a necessary work behind the scenes.

Keep your eyes on Me. I have begun a good work in you and I will bring it to completion.

MARCH 18

Daily Reading: John 10:1-16

John 10:4   And when he putteth forth his own sheep, he goeth before
them, and the sheep follow him: for they know his voice.

Listen to My voice and be sensitive to Me. It is easier to hear Me when it is something you want or desire, but when it is something you are not keen on then My voice gets questioned.

My sheep know My voice, and I will lead them through grassy fields to the still waters and also over the rocky terrain to get there. The road is My choosing, but I am always there to lead and guide you.

The more the shepherd has invested in the life of his sheep, the better he will take care of them. I have invested everything I have to the extent that I have given My very life for you. Do not I then desire the very best for you? Trust yourself completely to Me.

MARCH 19

Daily Reading: Genesis 50: 15-26

Genesis 50:17   *So shall ye say unto Joseph, Forgive, I pray thee now, the trespass of thy brethren, and their sin; for they did unto thee evil: and now, we pray thee, forgive the trespass of the servants of the God of thy father. And Joseph wept when they spake unto him.*

My child, I care for you and love you very much. My caring reaches out to all equally. My loving and caring nature wants to heal the hurts in My people. I desire that My people will have this same loving care for one another for by your love you shall be known.

To be able to love and care for each other there must first be forgiveness. I always forgive My people when they come to Me with a repentant heart. There is no limit to My forgiveness. As I show mercy, you must show mercy. I love you. Lay down your life for the brethren as I have laid down My life for you.

MARCH 20

Daily Reading: Luke 10:30-37

Luke 10:34   *And went to him, and bound up his wounds, pouring in oil and wine, and set him on his own beast, and brought him to an inn, and took care of him.*

I know your heart and the hurt you have in there. You have not done anything to bring this hurt your way. It was the enemy who attacked and wounded you. Release those hurts to Me and when you do, I can work on your behalf. I know your sorrows and heartache about this situation and I want to heal them. Give them to Me and I will pour in the oil and the wine.

Rejoice in Me and I will take this situation and turn it around for My glory. You will no longer have tears of hurt, but you will rejoice and have joy.

MARCH 21

Daily Reading: Luke 13:5-9

Psalm 1:3   *And he shall be like a tree planted by the rivers of water, that bringeth forth his fruit in his season; his leaf also shall not wither; and what soever he doeth shall prosper.*

Today is the first day of spring and that means new beginnings. The winter is past and the trees and plants are ready to start producing new growth again for another season. Your lives are like that also.

You have come through a season of winter where no one could see the growth taking place, but it was all happening in the root system.

My son, My daughter, you are entering a new season. The leaves are ready to start budding and men will see and rejoice. New growth will bring joy, promises of much fruit, and renewed vigor.

MARCH 22

Daily Reading: John 15

John 15:16   *Ye have not chosen Me, but I have chosen you, and ordained you, that ye should go and bring forth fruit, and that your fruit should remain:that whatsoever ye shall ask of the Father in My name, He may give it you.*

I have caused new growth to spring up in your root systems. Your roots have had to go down deep and tap into Me the Source, but now you are ready to start branching forth. The branches in you that do not produce fruit will be cut off. This is not meant to hurt you, but it will allow other branches to produce better quality fruit.

The world will pass by and they will notice the fruit. They may desire it, pass judgment on it or even condemn it, but remember the tree keeps on producing fruit. Rejoice in Me for the spring season of your life.

MARCH 23

Daily Reading: 1 Corinthians 13

1 Cor. 13:2b   *And though I have all faith, so that I could remove mountains, and have not charity (love), I am nothing.*

Love ministers many ingredients just like the sunshine has many nutrients that will give a healthy colour to a plant and its fruit. Without a lot of love in your life, your life will have no colour. Love is needed above all other ingredients. Sunshine without rain will scorch and burn things up. That is why we need the washing of God's Word. The washing that tears of repentance brings. Rain and sunshine both minister together.

Your appreciation of sunshine is much greater after a downpour then it was before. It is the same with My cleansing. You appreciate My love and the love of other Christians more after I have done a cleansing in your life. You will be able to soak up more love and you will stand out as a fresh healthy plant for Me and not as one that is shrivelled up and dying. A healthy plant with excellent fruit brings much glory to Me. Welcome the rain as much as the sunshine in your life.

MARCH 24

Daily Reading: Isaiah 1:16-20, Mark 7:1-23

Isaiah 1:16   *Wash you, make you clean; put away the evil of your doings from before Mine eyes; cease to do evil;*

I love you My child. I have given you this beautiful spring day. This is the time of the year that the grime, dirt and cobwebs from the winter and the past year are cleaned. I enjoy to see a clean wash blowing in my spring breezes. I desire the same for My people.

I desire to remove the grime and dirt from the past. I want My people to be washed by My blood and the reading of My word, and to be blown upon by the breezes of My Holy Spirit.

There are things in your life that need further cleansing and I desire to do this. Do not fear My cleansing, just keep your eyes on Me, rejoice in Me and trust

MARCH 25

Daily Reading: Psalm 5

Psalm 5:3   *My voice shalt Thou hear in the morning, O Lord; in the morning will I direct my prayer unto Thee, and will look up.*

I love you. I am with you for I live within you. That is a fact.

Do not let the busyness of the day overtake you before you spend time with Me. There is much I desire to share with you, but you must come and seek Me out and take the time to listen to Me. Many of My people are often too busy for Me and it grieves My heart for I have given sufficient hours in a day for everything to be accomplished. Rest in Me and do your work in My peace this day.

MARCH 26

Daily Reading: Joshua 2

Joshua 2:9   *And she said unto the men, I know that the Lord hath given you the land, and that your terror is fallen upon us, and that all the inhabitants of the land faint because of you.*

I love you so much. I am leading your lives. Do not concern yourself with what others think or say. You are in My will and I will bless you abundantly. My blessings will be an evident token of My love and My leading in your lives. To whomever it is important, it will be seen.

I open and I close eyes. All unbelief will keep your eyes closed. Learn to see My hand in everything. Acknowledge Me in all your ways and I will direct your ways. You must not be swayed by what you hear, but know in your heart that you are a part of Me and I cannot deny myself.

MARCH 27

Daily Reading: Romans 5:1-11

Romans 5:8   *But God commendeth His love toward us, in that, while we were yet sinners, Christ died for us.*

My child, I love you. Be encouraged this day. Do not start looking at what is not, but look to Me. Put down that desire that wants to tell everyone where you are at, but flow with the rest of the body for there must be unity in it.

You do not have to earn My love for My love is unconditional and it does not depend on feelings or actions. I love you because you have yielded yourself to Me. That is how you must love My body. Let My love flow through you to others.

MARCH 28

Daily Reading: Psalm 115

Psalm 115:15   *Ye are blessed of the Lord which made heaven and earth.*

I desire to see strongholds and principalities broken over your cities and in your lives. My children need to be set free so that they can more fully enter in to all that I have for them.

Praise Me for everything. Come into My presence with praise. Just knowing that I love you and care very much for you should set your soul rejoicing in praise and thankfulness.

I am in control of your life even to the extent that I have not lost count of the hairs on your head. You are special, you are loved and you are Mine.

MARCH 29

Daily Reading: Acts 9:1-22

Titus 2:14   *Who gave Himself for us, that He might redeem us from all iniquity, and purify unto Himself a peculiar people, zealous of good works.*

My child I gladly take all of your desires and ambitions. I will purify, change, and use you. Your old self has been constantly at war in you and with the desires I have placed in you. I have placed desires in your heart, but I can only use you when your heart is pure.

There can be no I dols in your heart for they will destroy you. Desiring

self-recognition will grow if left unchecked. All things should be done for Me and unto Me. I desire to lift you up, but I can only do this as you lift Me up.

With singleness of heart serve only Me. What is not of Me is either self or the enemy and both must be put to death. I love you My child.

MARCH 30

Daily Reading: Acts 6

Acts 6:3   *Wherefore, brethren, look ye out among you seven men of honest report, full of the Holy Ghost and wisdom, whom we may appoint over this business.*

Opportunities shall start coming your way. Seek Me much and I will lead you. Be faithful in the small things and I will open greater doors. Love one another with a pure heart. Purpose in your heart and in your mind to do all that I ask of you. I will be there to strengthen and equip you.

The time is now for I have opened doors and no man can shut them. Do not try to impress men, but just love and serve Me and I will make you known. Words will temporarily impress but it is how you love and serve Me that will speak. I will be with you this day.

MARCH 31

Daily Reading: Mark 4:35-41

Acts 27:22-24a.   *And now I exhort you to be of good cheer: for there shall be no loss of any man's life among you, but of the ship. For there stood by me this night the angel of God, whose I am, and whom I serve, Saying, Fear not,*

I am your captain and I go before you. I desire to go before you in all that you do. As captain of your souls I will lead you through the seas of life. There may be peace or storms may rage, but I am always in control of your ship. You need only rest in the fact that I am at the controls and in control.

I love you and I will lead and guide you this day.

APRIL 1

Daily Reading: Genesis 39, Psalm 105:16-22

Psalm 105:19   Until the time that His word came: the word of the Lord tried him.

You cannot see what I am doing now, but trust Me for my word will come to pass. All of self must be emptied out and gone. The foundations are being laid by Me and they are being built on Me, the solid rock. Keep your eyes on Me, not on your circumstances. Praise and rejoice in Me.

What I have said, I will do, for I cannot lie. I love you and I will make My way plain. I speak to My servants to love me, follow Me and obey Me. I am not requiring anything else. I will not lead you astray and you will not miss My timing. You are My beloved. I have called you and I will use you.

APRIL 2

Daily Reading: 1 John 4:7-21

1 John 4:18   There is no fear in love; but perfect love casteth out fear: because fear hath torment. He that feareth is not made perfect in love.

You do not trust Me completely. If you reason it out, you make your walk with Me difficult. I only desire the best for you. Let Me have the reins of your mind and will for you do not have to reason My ways out, or protect yourself, for I will protect you. I have shown you that I can do this. Just let go and let Me have the reins. I love you.

Do not fear Me, I will not let you down. Do not try to figure out all the answers to your questions and problems. Ask Me and I will tell you. I can do above and beyond anything you think you can figure out.

APRIL 3

Daily Reading: 2 Kings 4:8-37

2 Kings 4:26   *Run now, I pray thee, to meet her, and say unto her, Is it well with thee? is it well with thy husband? Is it well with the child? And she answered, It is well.*

Rejoice in me My son or daughter. I love you and I desire the best for you. I will take your hand in Mine as you walk with Me. Do not give in to anxious thoughts, but focus your mind on Me and fill it with Me. Past sins have been forgiven, and I remember them no more.

Rejoice in your husband, your wife, your sons and your daughters for they are my love gifts to you. I want to be with you, but many times you have missed Me because you have become too anxious. Just trust Me with the direction of your life. I desire only the best for you and those you love.

APRIL 4

Daily Reading: John 6:22-59

John 6:35   *And Jesus said unto them, I am the bread of life: he that cometh to Me shall never hunger; and he that believeth on Me shall never thirst.*

My child, I am your heavenly Father. I love you and I am watching over you like a father. I have your best interests at heart. I rejoice to see you seek Me, worship Me and grow closer to Me just as a father rejoices over growth in his children. It should be a natural part of life. When this does not happen, something is wrong.

Different things may stunt your growth. One could be lack of food and drink so drink deeply from Me, the Living water and feed on My Word, the *logos* and the *rhema*. You need My written word, but you also need the words that I have quickened to your heart in different ways. Be obedient to that word.

APRIL 5

Daily Reading: 2 Timothy 2:1-13

2 Timothy 2:4   *No man that warreth entangleth himself with the affairs of this life; that he may please him who hath chosen him to be a soldier.*

I am preparing you to do battle in My army. A soldier does not understand all the training, until he is in combat, when it will serve him well. A good soldier does not question his commanding officer, but obeys him.

Much is being prepared in the spiritual realm, which cannot be seen right now, but the fruit will show later. I am chipping away all doubts, fears and unbelief. If you could see the results now it would not build your faith and that is what I am building in you at this time. This training is not in vain. Only I can see the purpose of it and you must trust Me.

APRIL 6

Daily Reading: Genesis 28:10-21

Psalm 107:7   *And he led them forth by the right way, that they might go to a city of habitation.*

My child where I lead you, you have only but to follow. The one who leads takes all the obstacles out of the way and the one who follows does not have to do that. I am leading you in your work here and I am preparing the path for you to walk on.

Picture a rough wooded trail. The person who is leading will push the branches out of the way and if there are thorn bushes, he will hold them back and allow you to pass by. If there are rocks on the path, he will point them out to you. When you come to a bend where you can go no further, he will find an alternate route to get you to your destination.

I am leading and all you have to do is follow. Keep your eyes on Me and you will not stumble.

APRIL 7

Daily Reading: Daniel 3:1-30

Matt. 3:11b, 12   He shall baptize you with the Holy Ghost, and with fire: Whose fan is in his hand, and he will throughly purge his floor, and gather his wheat into the garner; but he will bum up the chaff with unquenchable fire.

Much has come against you, but I am keeping you. The fire shall not hurt you, no, not even the smell of smoke will cling to you. Walk in the ways that I have prepared for you and do not fall into the sin of unbelief. Confess Me before men and I will lift you up. Though a host of enemies come against you, do not look at them, but keep looking steadfastly to Me and I will not let you down.

No matter how difficult the trials, I will be with you this day.

APRIL 8

Daily Reading: Genesis 6:12-22

John 15:5   I am the vine, ye are the branches: He that abideth in Me, and I in him, the same bringeth forth much fruit: for without Me ye can do nothing.

I love you, My child. I am here ministering to your heart. Learn to let Me lead you. You have been taught independence. Some independence from people and situations is good, but not when it concerns Me. I am your supply of strength and I want to be everything to you.

Learn to let Me be a part of your daily routine, even as My Father was a part of My day, for I did nothing apart from My Father. I would seek Him in my quiet times and let Him tell Me what to do next, and how to do it. My word will tell you that apart from Me you can do nothing. Seek Me, draw close to Me and minister to Me.

APRIL 9

Daily Reading: 1 John 2:15-17, Romans 12:1-2

Psalm 106:15   *And He gave them their request; but sent leanness into their soul.*

I desire to be all of your life and I rejoice when My children seek to be totally yielded to My will. Many desire to do their own will and they want My blessing on it. When you desire to do My will, you will have My blessing on it.

My kingdom rules are not difficult, but your mind must let go of the way the world thinks. Listen to My Word for direction and guidance. My principles must become firmly planted in your heart, soul and mind. I live and breathe to do My Father's will.

Pray for My Holy Spirit to guide and illuminate My Word to you. If you seek My revelation and study My life as I walked this earth, you will discover new truths.

APRIL 10

Daily Reading: Psalm 23

1 Thess. 5:24   *Faithful is He that calleth you, who also will do it.*

Rest in Me and let Me lead and guide you. Learn to live each day as it comes and do not try to figure out what will come your way down the road.

You will be used in My kingdom. I have been preparing you all this time for a purpose. I have placed spiritual gifts within you and I will use you. People will not see you as you but as Me working through you. Do not look to yourself for it will discourage you, but look to Me.

I am blessing you and calling you. Rejoice in Me this day. I love you.

APRIL 11

Daily Reading: Psalm 91

Matthew 23:37   O Jerusalem, Jerusalem, thou that killest the prophets, and stonest them which are sent unto thee, how often would I have gathered thy children together, even as a hen gathered her chickens under her wings, and ye would not!

I look after My children so place your hand in Mine. I will protect and lead you. As long as you are hid in Me no harm can come to you. Many times I have sent angels to keep you from stumbling and from getting hurt.

You are special because you are My child. Every parent wants to protect His child and I am the same. I will protect you as long as you remain close to Me. Little chicks run into danger when they leave the protective covering of the hen's wings.

I love My children and My heart aches when they rebel and seek to do their own things, many times leaving themselves unprotected and open for attack. My ways are your protection. Do not try to reason things out for I can see pitfalls and obstacles ahead you cannot. I love you My child, stay close to Me this day.

APRIL 12

Daily Reading: Psalm 37

Psalm 37:4   Delight thyself also in the Lord; and He shall give thee the desires of thine heart.

I desire that My people come to Me, to worship Me, to bless Me and lift Me up. I am there for your needs but I desire your praise, adoration and worship from the heart. I desire for you to seek Me out. I desire for My children to think of Me above their own desires and needs. They will be met too, but I desire for you to worship and praise Me because I am your God.

When you yield everything completely to Me, I have no choice but to look after you. I desire to do this because I love you so much.

APRIL 13

Daily Reading: 2 Chronicles 16:11-14, 2 Kings 20: 1-7

3 John v.2   *Beloved, I wish above all things that thou mayest prosper and be in health, even as thy soul prospereth.*

When your will and your desires become as My will and My desires, you will prosper and be in health. Give yourself to My divine order. I love you and I will not ask anything of you that you are not able to do.

Do not fear physical ailments but command Satan to take his hands off your body for your whole being belongs to Me. I have placed My hedge of protection around you so use the authority I have given to you daily. Ask for My covering and My protection over you.

I rejoice in a thankful heart and attitude which expresses My person. No one was made to grumble for that is a negative spirit which is not from Me. Praise and thank Me for your health.

APRIL 14

Daily Reading: Genesis 1:26-31,2:1-8

Romans 8:19   *For the earnest expectation of the creature waiteth for the manifestation of the sons of God.*

There is much of My greatness that you have not yet seen or can even comprehend. As you give more of yourself to Me you will get to know more of Me and My greatness better.

I made this earth as a habitation for men to enjoy and rule. It is only in Me that men can have dominion on this earth. You must learn authority from Me for all creation is subject to My authority. At My command the mountains will move and the seas will dry up or change course. Man cannot understand, but I am the Lord that made all of this.

I am revealing more of Myself to you this day. I am in My creation and it shows forth My glory so show forth My glory this day!

APRIL 15

Daily Reading: 1 John 2:7-17

John 13:23   *Now there was leaning on Jesus' bosom one of His*
                    disciples, whom Jesus loved.

My child you often feel that there is so much that you must do, but the only thing I desire of you is that you remain close to Me, so close that you can hear Me even when I whisper. Be aware that activities can prevent you from hearing My voice.

My Son spent time apart with Me and in those times I ministered to Him. I gave Him direction and refreshed Him. He emptied Himself and I filled Him with My presence. As a result We became totally one.

I desire a continual closeness with you and with all My children, so do not hesitate to trust Me fully and completely. It does not matter if you understand everything but it does matter if you do not trust Me completely for I am your heavenly Father and I love you more than any earthly father.

APRIL 16

Daily Reading: Psalm 121

Luke 12:7   *But even the very hairs of your head are all numbered.*
                    Fear not therefore: ye are of more value than many
                    sparrows.

It was many a time during the night that My Son Jesus did not sleep, but instead He sought My presence and I would minister and speak to Him. I never sleep or slumber. I can refresh you without sleep. Do not be frustrated if you are unable to sleep but rejoice in Me.

This is the day that I have made! Listen to the birds outside, they know that their day has started and they are singing praises to Me. They are doing that which I have called them to do. There is no striving on their part, they just do it naturally. They are praising Me!

APRIL 17

Daily Reading: John 15:8-17

1 John 4:16   *And we have known and believed the love that God hath to us. God is love; and he that dwelleth in love dwelleth in God, and God in him.*

I love My people, but they cannot comprehend My love. It is not a human love which depends on responses and feelings, it is a love that keeps on ministering even when no one receives it. My love is an everlasting love which does not change. 1 cannot turn My love on and off. I AM LOVE. I am there to express Myself to you at all times.

As you draw closer to Me you will become more like Me and you will express more of My person to others. My child continue to draw closer and learn more about Me, and as you do, I will become a part of you. That is what becoming one with Me is all about.

APRIL 18

Daily Reading: 1 John 2:1-7

John 14:21   *He that hath My commandments, and keepeth them, he it is that loveth Me: and he that loveth Me shall be loved of My Father, and I will love him, and will manifest Myself to him.*

If you love Me, you will keep My commandments and obey Me. It is not good enough to say, "I love you," for all your words must be backed by your actions.

Spend as much time as you can with Me and saturate yourself with My Word for I desire that you enter into all the fullness that I have for you. Seek Me with all your heart, will and emotions. No man can take you away from Me, but your own will and mind can separate you from Me. You may not be aware of My presence but I am still hanging on to you. Seek My presence by commanding your will and mind to be set on Me. At times it may seem difficult but remember it only seems that way. I love you!

APRIL 19

Daily Reading: 1 Samuel 3

1 Samuel 3:10   *And the Lord came, and stood, and called as at other times, Samuel, Samuel. Then Samuel answered, Speak; for thy servant heareth.*

I love to speak to My sons and My daughters. Many times I am here to speak to My children but they are not there to listen. I will speak concerning the things to come, but My words do not need to be spoken over and over again. They will come to pass. It is My children who need to hear them over and over, so they will not forget but will continue to have faith and believe Me to bring them to pass. I speak to you through My prophets, My Word, the Bible, and I speak to your hearts as individuals.

Rejoice in Me this day. I will bless this day. I love you!

APRIL 20

Daily Reading: Hebrews 11:1-13

Hebrews 11:6   *But without faith it is impossible to please Him: for he that cometh to God must believe that He is, and that He is a rewarder of them that diligently seek Him.*

I love you both and I rejoice over what is happening in your lives. I see the desires in your hearts to be used by Me for My kingdom and My glory. That is My desire too. I have given you both many great and wonderful promises. These will not come to pass because you feel them, but because I spoke them and My Spirit will bring them to pass.

Your feet are planted on the rock. You may not always feel it, but that does not change the fact that it is there. I am that rock. As long as your eyes are focused on feelings they cannot be focused on Me. I do not move just because your emotions and feelings change. Praise Me much!

Daily Reading: Acts 4:1-4,13:44-52

Matthew 5:10 Blessed are they which are persecuted for righteousness' sake: for theirs is the kingdom of heaven.

I love to tell you that I love you for you are My beloved and I desire to be yours. You are a part of My kingdom and as you put Me first in every area of your life, all the time, you will receive more of My kingdom in your life.

Suffering for righteousness sake is part of being in My kingdom. I am working My fruit of righteousness in your life. You must continually put Me first in your thoughts and your eyes must remain upward. Your life is not your own it belongs to Me. My protection and provision is with you.

Daily Reading: Galatians 5:16-26

John 15:2 Every branch in Me that beareth not fruit He taketh away: and every branch that beareth fruit, He purgeth it, that it may bring forth more fruit.

I love you, My son and My daughter. I am pruning your lives to make you a better person and to produce larger fruit.

As the vine grows the gardener will prune back the branches to produce more excellent fruit. Things that were acceptable last year are no longer acceptable this year. Pruning hurts the tree and it may bleed a little, but sometimes the gardener puts a solution on the end of the branches that have been trimmed so that it will not hurt or affect the rest of the tree. Was that part of the branch which he cut off bad? No; but the gardener felt that by sacrificing a branch, the rest of the tree would grow stronger and produce more fruit.

You will be happier knowing that the gardener is happy with the fruit He is reaping for a tree is recognized by its fruit.

APRIL 23

Daily Reading: Isaiah 53

Matthew 5:44   *But I say unto you, Love your enemies, bless them that curse you, do good to them that hate you, and pray for them which despitefully use you, and persecute you;*

My daughter you have become very vulnerable. You have gone through much hurt and rejection, yet this was necessary so you would become the woman I ordained you to be.

I will bring healing to those hurts but this healing will be a process of time. I walked through all those hurts with you. When you were falsely accused, I was falsely accused, when you were put down, I was put down, when you were rejected, I was rejected. Do not try to protect yourself for it only causes hardness to be seen because a wall is being built, but be vulnerable for Me. Love the very ones who have hurt you, even if it means to be hurt again. It will be this quality and My love that will draw people to you.

APRIL 24

Daily Reading: Luke 4:14-30

Hebrews 12:3   *For consider Him that endured such contradiction of sinners against himself, lest ye be wearied and faint in your minds.*

My child, My arms are around you and I love you. You have been bombarded by hurts and rejections, negative thoughts and oppression, but I have not let you go. I was there all the time, but you did not focus on Me, you focused on your hurt feelings. I was rejected and talked about by the church leaders. They did not believe Me, and I am the very God that they professed to serve.

My child rejections and hurts will come, but I will never hurt or reject you, for I am here to heal and restore you. You know these things in your head, but they must rule your heart. I will hold you close to My heart this day.

APRIL 25

Daily Reading: James 4

James 4:8   *Draw nigh to God, and He will draw nigh to you. Cleanse*
                 your hands, ye sinners; and purify your hearts, ye double
                 minded.

I love you My child, and I see the turmoil and the contradictory thoughts. One minute they are for Me and the next minute they are against My people. This cannot be. I love you and I love them and I hurt when you hurt or when they hurt. I desire for your mind to be occupied with Me this day.

Negative thoughts are a destructive tool from the enemy, so keep your eyes on Me and you will be able to see everything in perspective. The enemy is about to be rooted out and he is doing everything he can to prevent that from happening. I have placed My hedge around you and you must speak the word of faith and command him to leave.

APRIL 26

Daily Reading: John 14:21-31

John 3:16   *For God so loved the world, that He gave his only begotten*
                 Son, that whosoever believeth in Him should not perish,
                 but have everlasting life.

I love you My son and My daughter. It is good to tell those you love each day that you love them. This builds up a person and causes a loving and secure relationship.

Rejection cannot minister when a person is secure in the fact that they are loved. My people are loved by Me, but many do not hear Me saying it to them. Their ears are not open to Me, their heavenly Father, but rather they are listening to other voices in their mind.

I love My people and I love you. With Me, each one of My children is special. The enemy is at work spreading seeds of rejection, insecurities and fears, but perfect love casts out all fears. Receive My love and give it to others.

APRIL 27

Daily Reading: 1 Samuel 1:1-18, 2:1-11

> *1 Samuel 2:1*   *And Hannah prayed, and said, My heart rejoiceth in the Lord, mine horn is exalted in the Lord: my mouth is enlarged over mine enemies; because I rejoice in Thy salvation.*

I desire the worship and praise of My people. for it expresses their love to Me. You love to hear it when someone says that they love you and that is what your worship and praise says to Me. My heart rejoices when My people express themselves in this way.

I love you My child, and whoever attacks you unjustly attacks Me in you. You do not have to defend yourself, for I will defend you. Praise Me for what I am going to do and praise Me for what I have done. Rejoice in Me this day!

APRIL 28

Daily Reading: Jonah 1 & 2

> *Job 1:10*   *Hast not Thou made an hedge about him, and about his house, and about all that he hath on every side? Thou hast blessed the work of his hands, and his substance is increased in the land.*

Live in a thankful attitude for when you are grumbling and complaining it is not the situation, but Me you are complaining about, for I ordained and planned your life. When something happens that you do not like you complain about it because you do not like the fact that I allowed this to come your way.

Thank Me and praise Me that I am in control of your life and all situations, rather than Satan. He has gained access to many people's wills and emotions and so he has them obeying him instead, but this is not so in your life for I am in control and I have placed My hedge around you to protect you.

APRIL 29
Daily Reading: Luke 24:13-33

Luke 24:17   And He said unto them, What manner of communications are these that ye have one to another, as ye walk, and are sad?

I love you, My child. Walk in My ways this day and give no place to any negative thoughts, but keep your mind on Me.

There is a preparation going on in your life for I am going to use you. I do not prepare people without a reason so remain close to Me and obey Me and I will lead you into new things. I am the potter and I am shaping you into a vessel fit for the master's use. Do not give way or room to discouragement for you know that it is not from Me.

There are many who need to be taught My ways and I will use you to teach them. The road may be long, but I am walking it with you.

APRIL 30
Daily Reading: Romans 7

Romans 7:22   For I delight in the law of God after the inward man.

My daughter I love you. I know you better than anyone else does. I designed you. I made you. I even know you better than you know yourself.

In certain areas of your life you must enter into more discipline for your heart desires after Me, but at times other things take priority. I enjoy these times we spend together, and they can grow.

I have a storehouse of treasures that you have not even begun to tap into and I desire to show them to you. Do not compare yourself with anyone else, but look only to Me.

MAY 1

Daily Reading: Philippians 3: 1-9

Proverbs 14:26   In the fear of the Lord is strong confidence: and his children shall have a place of refuge.

Bring all your questions to Me. You want so much to hear approval coming from people, when the only approval you need is My approval. I am pleased with you.

You are afraid to express with confidence what I am doing in your lives because you have let fear minister to you. Share with confidence that I am leading you and your confidence in Me will minister to others. You must trust Me in whatever I lead you to do.

Rejoice in Me this day as you do your work My approval is the only approval, and My provision is the only provision you will need. In Me are all your answers.

MAY 2

Daily Reading: Genesis 45: 1-15

Isaiah 30:15   For thus saith the Lord God, the Holy One of Israel; In returning and rest shall ye be saved; in quietness and in confidence shall be your strength: and ye would not.

I love you so rest in Me and let all things come to rest. Focus your eyes on Me and as you look to Me the things of this earth will grow strangely dim. I am leading you, but if you focus your eyes on things around you, you will question and not see My hand in it at all. I am not leading you astray for I go before you and you can rest in the fact that you are in My will. Satan wants to rob you of the joy of being in My will. Do not be discouraged, but let your heart be encouraged, because I am bringing to pass your hopes and expectations.

MAY 3

Daily Reading: Joshua 6

*Isaiah 57: 13b-14 But he that putteth his trust in Me shall possess the land,
and shall inherit My holy mountain; And shall say, Cast
ye up, cast ye up, prepare the way, take up the stumbling
block out of the way of My people.*

I can do above and beyond anything you can imagine. I am able to cause miracles to happen in your favour that the world would be amazed at. I am not stopped by financial limitations as I own everything.

Start speaking forth the promises that I have given to you. You will see people set free, strongholds broken down and families turned around and joined together in Me. Speak these things and don't try to figure them out for I will do it. I just need a heart of thanksgiving proclaiming My promises and praising Me for them.

Would you deny a gift to someone after you had told them they were going to receive it and they were thanking and praising you for it? No, neither would I. I love you more and I cannot lie.

MAY 4

Daily Reading: Genesis 15

*Romans 4:20,21 He staggered not at the promise of God through unbelief;
but was strong in faith, giving glory to God; And being fully
persuaded that, what He had promised, He was able also
to perform.*

My child, following Me by walking in faith is not difficult. When you look through natural eyes it seems difficult, but when you keep your eyes on Me it is not for your total dependance is then on Me and I will have to answer your prayers and fulfill your desires.

Walking by faith means defying the natural ways and means to obtain the promises, coming to rest and letting Me answer and work it out. You rest and I will do the work. Stop expressing negative attitudes and just thank Me for that which I am going to do. Voice your thanksgiving and praise! As you believe. this, you will share with others the things I am going to do in your life. Rest in Me and I will do the work.

MAY 5

Daily Reading: Matthew 11:28-30, Luke 2:40-52

Matthew 11:29a. Take My yoke upon you, and learn of Me;

Hebrews 5:8   Though He were a Son, yet learned He obedience by the things which He suffered;

My yoke is easy and My burden is light, so let Me teach you. Many people forget the last part for they do not want to go through the learning experience. You cannot expect to run before you have first of all learned to crawl and then learned to walk. It is this way in My kingdom, so let Me teach you. I am not a hard teacher. I am there to pick you up when you fall, and My love is continually watching over you to protect you. I hurt when you hurt, but I look beyond that hurt and see you accomplishing great things.

When you yield yourself to the training it is not difficult, but when you go against the training the way becomes hard. Do not fear a learning process for fear will paralyze and prevent you from moving on. When you trust Me completely, your burden will be light because it will not be you carrying the burden but Me, and that is what makes it so light. Rejoice and give thanks to Me.

MAY 6

Daily Reading: Acts 27

Acts 27:34   *Wherefore I pray you to take some meat: for this is for*
                    your health: for there shall not an hair fall from the head
                    of any of you.

Lord do You have a word in the storm?

I have taken your hand and you are under My protective covering. Release your praises to Me. The storms may come and rage, but I will be in the boat with you, and you will be able to trample the enemy under your feet, for your feet are shod with the gospel of peace. Your righteousness is of Me. You have been set free by Me. No enemy can touch you, for I am hanging on to you. It is not you that is being attacked, but Me. Darkness cannot tolerate the light and My light is shining through you. Remember I am by your side and I love you.

MAY 7

Daily Reading: 1 Peter 3:1-6

Genesis 2: 18   *And the Lord God said, It is not good that the man should*
                    be alone; I will make him an help meet for him.

My daughter be assured this day that I love you very much.

Rejoice in your husband. Be excited with him for I have called you to be a help meet to him. I will bless him abundantly for I am filling him with My storehouse of knowledge of Me. He will love you. Try to please him and let him tell you what pleases him. Lift him up for he is your head. Serve him and always desire the best for him. Stand by your husband and pray for him. Tell him you love him. I have ordained for you two to be together and I am making you one. He is my love gift to you.

MAY 8

Daily Reading: Ephesians 5:22-33

I Corinthians 11:3 But I would have you know, that the head of every man is Christ; and the head of the woman is the man; and the head of Christ is God.

I love you. I desire for My will to be done in your life and I desire to bring you to new heights in Me.

Obey those that have the rule over you and you will walk in My ways. I have created divine order, it is in My word. I will not go against My word, so relax in that fact. Your own thinking may be wrong, but the order of My word is not.

Trust in your husband, for he is your head and your protector. Satan would have you bypass him in decisions. It would seem very spiritual the other way, especially when I may have given you a revelation or insight into something. You may share this information with him, but then you must submit to your husband's desires, for I have given him to you and he is able to hear from Me.

I will speak clearly to him and direction for your lives will come through him. I will use the order I have set forth. Rest in Me and in your husband.

MAY 9

Daily Reading: Psalm 128

I Peter 3:7   *Likewise, ye husbands, dwell with them according to knowledge, giving honour unto the wife, as unto the weaker vessel, and as being heirs together of the grace of life; that your prayers be not hindered.*

I love you both and you are special to Me. You have been called to stand together as husband and wife. I am continuing my work in both of you to make you one. When you are one, you will be in perfect agreement.

I am getting rid of the uncleanness in your hearts. More of My power and love can flow through you when you are in total unity together and I can use you in a greater way. One can put a thousand to flight, but two, ten thousand and this does not just double, it multiplies. I will bless you both this day!

MAY 10

Daily Reading: Matthew 6: 19-34

Colossians 3:2   *Set your affection on things above, not on things on the earth.*

My child, do not be so concerned with temporal things such as the fashions of this world, but set your affections on heavenly things, where moth and rust will not corrupt. I will provide all those things you have need of when you look to Me, for I want to bless you abundantly. The fashions of this world are here today and gone tomorrow and have no lasting effect. Trust Me for I know what you have need of.

Do not give so much time dwelling on the other things in your mind. They go over and over in your mind. Instead, rejoice and rest in Me for I want to see you looking nice too. I am not only concerned with outward beauty, but I also desire beauty in your innermost being. When you rest in Me, it will bring inner beauty because you are meditating and feeding on Me. What then is inside will show on the outside also. Be beautiful for Me, as I your heavenly Father delight in you. Let Me truly provide for all of your needs.

MAY 11

Daily Reading: John 12:23-36

Psalm 37:23,24   The steps of a good man are ordered by the Lord: and He delighted in his way. Though he fall, he shall not be utterly cast down, for the Lord upholdeth him with His hand.

I love you My son and My daughter. You need My word daily. I want to spend time with you and go before you each day for it will make your day so much easier. I will be here this day, rejoice before Me.

Your steps have been ordered by Me. Let Me lead you and let My joy be your strength. Praise Me and listen to My word. Obey My word and minister it to others. When My word has become life to you, you can then speak it with authority to others. When a seed dies, I then give it new life to grow again and it will give expression of life in many different forms. So it is with My word in your life. When it becomes life to you it will be an expression of life to others in many different ways.

MAY 12

Daily Reading: 1 Corinthians 6:12-20

Psalm 103:12   As far as the east is from the west, so far hath He removed our transgressions from us.

I have forgiven you all your sins and unrighteousness and I see you as a clean vessel before Me.

Put your flesh under subjection. You must learn to rule it and not let the desires of your flesh rule you. I am your strength and your guide. All things are lawful, but not all things are expedient. Relax in Me and keep your heart and mind fixed on Me. I love you and when I forgive, I remember your sins no more. More and more you must let Me rule in your heart, soul, mind and flesh for I desire to pour out My blessings upon you.

MAY 13

Daily Reading: Mark 4:1-20

Luke 11:10,13b   *For every one that asketh receiveth; and he that seeketh findeth; and to him that knocketh it shall be opened. How much more shall your heavenly Father give the Holy Spirit to them that ask Hint?*

I love you and I will bring rains of refreshing and renewing to pour down on you for they are needed on the earth. Seeds have been planted within you and I will rain upon them and cause them to shoot forth and grow. After a spring rain you can almost see the garden and lawn grow. The rains will come down upon you and there will be great time of growing.

Ask Me to refresh you and to pour My Spirit out on you in a greater measure than ever before. Ask Me to change you more into My likeness and as you ask, I will answer, but first you must ask Me.

MAY 14

Daily Reading: Luke 15:11-32

1 Peter 1:22   *Seeing ye have purified your souls in obeying the truth through the Spirit unto unfeigned love of the brethren, see that ye love one another with a pure heart fervently:*

I rejoice when I am told that I am loved. We all need love and acceptance from others and that is why you need to love and encourage My people. Many have not had true love and acceptance in their life, and because of this they cannot understand that I can love them and accept them exactly as they are.

Many people have a distorted view of what I am really like because they compare Me to their own standards. My standards are far greater. I am love and acceptance.

When a certain ingredient is missed while baking a cake, it will have a drastic result on the finished product. When the yeast is left out, the cake remains small and hard, but with the yeast, it bakes up high and light and fluffy. When it is not baked properly it is too heavy to eat and the stomach finds it hard to digest. So it is with My love. When things come your way, just knowing that My love and acceptance is mixed in it, makes it easier to eat and digest.

MAY 15

Daily Reading: Colossians 1:1-14

Colossians 1:9   *For this cause we also, since the day we heard it, do not cease to pray for you, and to desire that ye might be filled with the knowledge of His will in all wisdom and spiritual understanding;*

My children, I love you very much and I desire and seek your closeness. When you are very close to Me, you will hear My heartbeat which is My desire for my children. Every father has desires and hopes for his children. I am no different, I have great hopes and desires for My children. Just stay close and seek My fellowship and I will share some of these things with you.

I love you My children. You have been called and appointed by Me to bear much fruit. I will rejoice over you.

MAY 16

Daily Reading: Jeremiah 18:1-10

Ephesians 2: 10   *For we are His workmanship, created in Christ Jesus unto good works, which God hath before ordained that we should walk in them.*

You are My workmanship and there is nothing you can do to change yourself. Only I can change hearts. Changes must come from the inside first, then the outward for only then will they last. Man can change his outward appearance but it will not last.

You are My workmanship, and this means I will change you the way I want you to be. Be like the lump of clay on the potter's wheel. It does not fight the potter, but it willingly submits itself. I want to make you into a beautiful vessel for My purposes. I want to take pleasure in you. Willingly submit to changes, I take pleasure in My workmanship. I rejoice in you. Rejoice in Me this day!

MAY 17

Daily Reading: Isaiah 42: 1-12

Isaiah 42:1a   *Behold My servant, whom I uphold; Mine elect, in whom My soul delighteth;*

Psalm 147:6   *The Lord lifteth up the meek: He casteth the wicked down to the ground.*

You are My child and I desire to lift you up. I desire to lift all My children up so that the world may know that these are My children. I love them and I am proud of them for they love and serve Me. They are My lights in this world.

There is so much of this world still living in darkness that has yet to receive My light. They do not realize that things could be different. I desire for them to know this, but it is My children who must tell them. As they lift Me up, I will lift them up to be a bright light to those around them. My children can only shine brightly when all of the dark areas in their lives have been cast down.

My heart aches for the multitudes that are crying out for help and do not know where to turn. I desire for My people to reach out and touch them.

MAY 18

Daily Reading: 2 Kings 6:8-23

Proverbs 3:5,6   *Trust in the Lord with all thine heart; and lean not unto thine own understanding. In all thy ways acknowledge Him, and He shall direct thy paths.*

My ways are always before you and I desire that you walk in My paths. Whatever you do will constantly be watched by others for they will be watching you to see if you slip. I do not want you to think about that; instead ask yourself if you are pleasing to God. When you know you are pleasing Me others cannot help but notice that you are walking in the light.

When you please Me you will be an example and a light for Me. Forgive others quickly and run to Me with every situation. I am pleased when you acknowledge Me in all your ways. When things are given to Me I can turn them around. I can turn curses into blessings.

MAY 19

Daily Reading: Acts 17:16-34

Matthew 7:6   *Give not that which is holy unto the dogs, neither cast ye your pearls before swine, lest they trample them under their feet, and turn again and rend you.*

Enter into My rest this day and let Me lead and guide you in everything you do. Be sensitive to what I would have you share with others.

Seeds cannot be planted until the ground has first been prepared. I, the Lord, prepare the soil of hearts, but I can only do this as hearts are yielded to Me. Do not force new things (seeds) into hearts that have not been prepared for them yet. As you listen for My direction, My Spirit will guide you.

MAY 20

Daily Reading: John 4:19-26

Psalm 99:5   *Exalt ye the Lord our God, and worship at His footstool; for He is holy.*

Zephaniah 3:17 *The Lord thy God in the midst of thee is mighty; He will save, He will rejoice over thee with joy; He will rest in His love, He will joy over thee with singing.*

I am rejoicing in the praises of My people. It is sweet music to My ears. From all over the world it harmonizes together before My throne. When My people worship Me in spirit and in truth, it is an acceptable offering before Me and a sweet smelling sacrifice. If it does not come from the heart it is an offensive odor to me and is dead, something that is dead stinks.

I desire to give new life and to quicken people. I the Lord can quicken, change and renew lives. Enjoy this day in fellowship with Me and with each other. I love you!

MAY 21

Daily Reading: Luke 9:57-62, 1 Kings 19:19-21

Hebrews 12:2   *Looking unto Jesus the author and finisher of our faith;*
who for the joy that was set before Him endured the cross,
despising the shame, and is set down at the nght hand of
the throne of God.

No man putting his hand to the plow and looking back is worthy of My kingdom, so look ahead to Me, the author and finisher of your faith. Keep your eyes steadfastly on Me, or you will miss many things. Do not look back but press ahead. Many things are happening even this day among My people, but those who are not looking for it, will not see it. It was the same in Jesus' day. When people were looking for the kingdom of God, Jesus told them, "It is among you." It is the same today.

Look unto Me this day and I will bless your day.

MAY 22

Daily Reading: 1 John 3: 1-12

Luke 2:49   *And He said unto them, How is it that ye sought Me? Wist*
ye not that I must be about My Father's business?

You are My son. You started out being My child, but now you have matured into sonship and its responsibilities.

I have shown you from My word that Jesus spent much time seeking Me for his daily direction. Learn to recognize My heartbeat and remain close to Me for I have much work that needs to be done.

I need My church to rise up and take their place of authority. My word declares, "greater things than these shall ye do", and it is so. Can you picture what will happen when every believer walks in My authority? Satan will be defeated and there will be no room for him to move. Then will I be exalted!

MAY 23

Daily Reading: Romans 6

Romans 6:13   Neither yield ye your members as instrnments of unrighteousness unto sin: but yield yourselves unto God, as those that are alive from the dead, and your members as instruments of righteousness unto God.

Put off that which is not of Me, for your life is dead and you are hid in Me. Do not keep on feeding something that is dead.

Since your life is hid in Me, I will protect with My life all that you have placed in My care. Your striving should be in putting to death the wrong desires and wrong things that minister to a dead body. They stink because they minister death rather than life.

Your life is hid in Me, and it has a sweet fragrance because you have abundant life. Your old life was nailed to the cross and put to death. When I was nailed to the cross I arose in newness of life from the grave. It is not enough to bring wrong thoughts and deeds to the cross to be put to death, you need to bury them in the grave forever. When they are left out in plain sight they will stink and be offensive to all who view them. I love you. Your life is hid in Me!

MAY 24

Daily Reading: Galatians 6

Galatians 6:4,9   But let every man prove his own work, and then shall he have rejoicing in himself alone, and not in another. And let us not be weary in well doing: for in due season we shall reap, if we faint not.

I love you, and I rejoice in your thankful heart. I have set you free by My grace, love and mercy. It does not depend on you but it is all My doings. Show to others what I have shown to you and love others as I love you. Minister in My name to others as I have ministered to you.

I am very much at work in your life. You may think I have passed you by, but that is not so. I am watching over you and I am at work on your behalf. I have called you and nothing goes on in your life that I do not know about or allow. Praise Me much. Rejoice over what I am doing, even this day!

MAY 25

Daily Reading: Revelation 2

Rev. 2:26,27   *And he that overcometh, and keepeth My works unto the end, to him, will I give power over the nations: And he shall nile them with a rod of iron; as the vessels of a potter shall they be broken to shivers: even as I received of My Father.*

I love My people very much, and I see the things which are tormenting them. I want to set them free, but many times they are unaware of the real problem. I have to surface it and show them so they can be set free, purified and cleansed.

I see that My people are ensnared, bound up and some are totally taken captive, but My heart's desire is to see them set free. I do not delight in curses, but in blessings.

I have given authority to My church to set the captives free and as I lead, you must do this. Our warfare is not against flesh and blood, but against the strongholds in the heavenlies. I am expectantly waiting for My church to rise up and take her stand.

MAY 26

Daily Reading: Isaiah 5:1-16

Isaiah 5:4, 13a   *What could have been done more to My vineyard, that I have not done in it? Wherefore, when I looked that it should bringforth grapes, brought it forth wild grapes? Therefore My people are gone into captivity, because they have no knowledge:*

I love you My child, and My dealings are a form of expressing My love to you.

The gardener that loves his orchard will take care of his trees. He will remove the boulders, which have been there a long time and prevented growth, from around the roots of the trees by casting them away. Satan is like the boulders in that he would try to rob us of our nourishment and must be cast out. Weeds have a tendency to spring up quickly. They too are the work of the enemy as they try to choke the roots. The stronger the roots of the tree the less effect those weeds will have. Weeds are like the influences of the world. In a young plant they do real harm but as the tree grows and spreads its branches and leaves, those weeds will be snuffed out.

Rejoice over the dealings in your life for they show how much I care and that I desire the best for you. You are a tree in My orchard. Praise Me this day!

MAY 27

Daily Reading: Job 42

Job 3:25   *For the thing which I greatly feared is come upon me, and that which I was afraid of is come unto me.*

Put aside your fear that more hurts will come your way, for I am a healer and a restorer. I do not hurt any of My children willfully. I want to heal your hurts.

I am pleased with your life and I am pleased that you desire My will in it. I can turn around every situation and use every obstacle that Satan has placed in your way to hinder or hurt your walk with Me. When I turn the situation around, it will bring praise and glory to Me. Do not fear any confrontation, for the only thing that can get hurt is the outward man and he must die anyway.

Keep your eyes on Me. Think on Me. My hand is on you for good. I love you.

MAY 28

Daily Reading: Psalm 119:129-144

Ps. 119:167, 168   *My soul hath kept Thy testimonies; and I love them exceedingly. I have kept Thy precepts and Thy testimonies: for all my ways are before Thee.*

I am here beside you and I love you. My presence will continually go with you. There is not a thing that goes on in your lives that I am not aware of.

I see your desire to love and serve Me. Enter more into prayer and praise Me much. Share with others what I am doing in your lives and let it be a testimony unto Me. There are many ways your light can shine unto Me. Enter into all that I have shown you. More and more of My riches are becoming a part of you.

Rejoice in Me this day, I will be with you.

MAY 29

Daily Reading: Psalm 145

Acts 15:4   *And when they were come to Jerusalem, they were received of the church, and of the apostles and elders, and they declared all things that God had done with them.*

You are My child and I love you. Your strength, your help and your hope is in Me. Everything that you are and will be is in Me. I am your all and in all. I will be with you this day and My blessing is upon you. Rejoice in Me!

Testify of my goodness and faithfulness. I love My people and desire to meet their needs. They must come to Me and seek Me to do this. Let My glory shine through you today. My people are the only ones through whom this can happen. Think of Me, speak of Me, and rejoice in Me.

MAY 30

Daily Reading: Mark 6:32-46

Numbers 14:8   *If the Lord delight in us, then He will bring us unto this land, and give it us; a land which floweth with milk and honey.*

I love you and you are a partaker of My kingdom. You are a part of My world rather than the world you live in. Whatever you do is for My glory and as you do it unto Me, I will bless it.

I delight to feed My people. I delight in speaking to them and ministering to them. I have always desired that My people's hearts be totally turned and yielded to Me.

I delight in your praises and as you praise Me, My glory will be you. Rejoice in Me this day!

MAY 31

Daily Reading: Esther 6

Proverbs 3:24   *When thou liest down, thou shalt not be afraid: yea, thou shalt lie down, and thy sleep shall be sweet.*

I give My beloved sleep, but even without sleep I can give rest to your body. There is one called, the "robber of sleep", which is the adversary, who would not have you sleep. I have made the night for sleeping, but the enemy would reverse that and do all his activity at night.

There are times when I will wake My children at night to speak to them, but they will know it is Me that wake them up. When the enemy wakes you up, or keeps you awake, focus on Me. As you commune with Me, you will defeat his purposes. This will thwart him and it will give you a rejoicing spirit. My peace will rule in the situation.

I desire that you have a good day in me. Praise Me much.

JUNE 1

Daily Reading: Matthew 2:12-23

Matthew 2:13a   *And when they were departed, behold the angel of the*
Lord appeareth to Joseph in a dream, saying, Arise, and
take the young Child and His mother, and flee into Egypt,
and be thou there until I bring thee word:

My son, My daughter, I love you. Do not allow fear to set into your heart. Do not fear that you have made a wrong move, you haven't. Your move is in My perfect will and timing for you both. Now was your time to move on.

As you seek Me and are willing to lay all else aside and to do what I will show you and not what man will try to show you, then you will hear clearly from Me. It is important that you keep your eyes focused on Me and not on man. I will not lead you astray. My purpose for your life is the best for My desire for you is only to give you My very best.

JUNE 2

Daily Reading: 2 Chronicles 32:1-22

2 Chron. 32:7,8a   *Be strong and courageous, be not afraid nor dismayed for*
the king of Assyria, nor for all the multitude that is with
him: for there be more with us than with him: With him is
an arm of flesh; but with us is the Lord our God to help us,
and to fight our battles.

You have been called by Me to have a special place in My kingdom. Our fight is not with flesh and blood, but with principalities and powers. My power is stronger and I will prevail.

You shall trample the enemy under your feet, but remember to keep your eyes on Me, I am your captain. Without Me you are powerless so let Me fill you with My power and use you. Light will win for My host is at your disposal to help you; just call on My name. As captain over you, I send you forth and cover for you. When you are under My command you are under My protection and the strongholds shall be broken and defeated.

I the Lord of host have spoken it and it will be accomplished. Great victory will be yours.

JUNE 3

Daily Reading: Joshua 1

Deut. 28:12   *The Lord shall open unto thee His good treasure, the heaven to give the rain unto thy land in His season, and to bless all the work of thine hand: and thou shalt lend unto many nations, and thou shalt not borrow.*

The wilderness journey is over. The manna from the desert will stop and the fruit of the land will be yours. Can you imagine how the Israelites must have felt as they stood at the Jordan ready to enter the promised land, the land of their dreams and promises. They could hardly believe that there would be no more wandering in the desert, but a settling down in a new home. They could not even imagine it.

My promises to Joshua went before the Israelites and My promises to you are going before you. Be strong and of good courage, for I go before you and I will bless you. Do not be afraid for I will be there to lead and guide you.

JUNE 4

Daily Reading: 1 Samuel 16:14-23

Proverbs 18:16   *A man's gift maketh room for him, and bringeth him before great men.*

I am your Lord and King and I love you. You think negative thoughts about yourself, but I do not think those things. You have known My chastening hand and My teaching hand but I am about to do a new thing. My hand of blessing will be upon you. Where you have been put down I will raise you up.

My Word says, "A man's gift will make room for him." I have given you gifts and I will make room for them. They are first of all given to bring glory and honour to Me and My name. Your expectations will be met. I have invested much in you and it has not been in vain. There will come forth much fruit.

JUNE 5

Daily Reading: Isaiah 60

*Philippians 2: 15   That ye may be blameless and harmless, the sons of God,
without rebuke, in the midst of a crooked and perverse
nation, among whom ye shine as lights in the world;*

I desire for you to be a channel through which My light can flow. All things come from and return to Me. I want you to be a light for Me. In order for the moon to reflect light to the earth it must stay in orbit with the sun. You must stay close by My side and follow Me just the same. My fragrance must permeate you, so that it will be noticed on you.

Keep your eyes on Me and do not let Satan rob your thought life by focusing on people or situations. Bring all such thoughts into captivity and give them to Me. Do not even entertain them, for in so doing you will be affected by them, and that is what the enemy of your soul is trying to do.

JUNE 6

Daily Reading: Psalms 149

*Psalm 100:2   Serve the Lord with gladness: come before His presence
with singing.*

Sing praises unto Me!

I have given you your voice, and I love to hear you sing. It thrills My heart. When I place gifts within My people, I also make a way possible for these gifts to be a blessing unto Me and unto others. I have placed gifts within you, not to be a storehouse but to be a channel for Me to flow through to others.

Keep your eyes on Me and watch Me open doors for ministry. When I say to someone I will open a door, you do not have to pound it from the other side, just sit back and wait for it to be opened. When it is open get up and walk through it and give Me all the glory!

JUNE 7
Daily Reading: Acts 16:25-34

Psalm 146:2 *While I live will I praise the Lord: I will sing praises unto My God while I have any being.*

Your praises minister to Me. When you praise Me you put your own desires aside and you think of Me. I desire your praises. I can give you anything your heart desires, even without you asking Me for it, but the. one thing you can give Me is your praises for only My people can give Me that. That is why it means so much to Me.

The world cannot praise Me from the heart. They may be forced to worship Me at times but only someone whose heart is right with Me can worship Me in spirit and in truth. The one thing that makes man different from the animals is that I gave man a free will. They can choose of themselves to praise Me, animals cannot.

I love to hear the praises of My people. You will see that every new move of God is accompanied by new songs and praises being written and sung.

Enjoy My presence this day. Give Me your praises, I desire to delight in you this day.

JUNE 8 *Abby/Kate*
Daily Reading: Luke 13:10-17

2 Corinthians 1:4 *Who comforteth us in all our tribulation, that we may be able to comfort them which ate in any trouble, by the comfort wherewith we ourselves are comforted of God.*

I have not made one person to be like another one, and there are needs in each person's life. Those needs are there, so they will call upon Me. I use that to draw them to Myself. It is love that reaches out to those needs.

I have placed My love in you so use that love to minister to people's needs. Do not be intimidated by people for that is only a cover up that they try and use to make themselves look good.

Many people feel they cannot let their real needs be shown. It is not them. Satan has convinced them not to reveal that side of themselves because if they did it would show that they were less of a Christian than the other people. That is a lie. Ask Me to show you what their needs are. I want to help people.

JUNE 9

Daily Reading: Luke 7:36-50

1 John 4:7   *Beloved, let us love one another:for love is of God; and*
                    everyone that loveth is born of God, and knoweth God.

The church must minister My love and acceptance. My people are the church. They must believe first that I am, who I say I am and second that I love My people unconditionally. When this becomes a reality in their own lives, they will then be able to minister it to others.

Love must come from the heart. Words can be empty. Faith without works is dead likewise love without the heart is dead. Some people will be difficult to love. The very thing they need, they push away. They have only known one thing, and that is rejection. They can only respond with what they know, rejection. I want to see My people set free from this rejection. They need to know I love them and that I will not reject them.

Pray for discernment to see people as I see them, to have My heart of love ministering and flowing through you. I love you and I will be with you today.

JUNE 10

Daily Reading: 2 Timothy 2:14-23

I Cor. 13:12   *For now we see through a glass, darkly; but then face to face: Now I know in part; but then shall I know even as also I am known.*

I love you, My child. You desire to see Me with your natural eye, but that is not necessary. I live in you. I love you and I have taken control of your life.

You seek to do My will and you will when all your desires for self are laid on the altar. You are being emptied of self to be an empty vessel that I can fill for My use and purposes. When much preparation goes into a vessel it means it will be a special vessel for a special purpose.

JUNE 11

Daily Reading: Psalm 133

Mark 8:33b   *Get thee behind Me, Satan: for thou savourest not the things that be of God, but the things that be of men.*

Your enemy is at work. He desires to destroy you and get you to disagree. In unity with Me you are mighty, but when you are divided you cannot stand. Look to Me, let Me control and regulate your life, even your life with one another. I can make your plans one. Satan is the accuser of the brethren. Do not listen to those negative thoughts in your mind and do not listen to the negative reports about your brethren.

Focus your eyes on Me. I am in control and I will lead you and guide you because you are Mine and I love you. Listen to My voice this day and you will have My peace within you.

JUNE 12

Daily Reading: 2 Corinthians 10

Philippians 4:8   *Finally, brethren, whatsoever things are true, whatsoever things are honest, whatsoever things are just, whatsoever things are pure, whatsoever things are lovely, whatsoever things are of good report; if there be any virtue, and if there be any praise, think on these things.*

Your thought life must be given to Me all the time. Many ideas enter into your head and you dwell on them first, before you consider whether or not they are of Me. First consider whether they are of Me and if they are not, rebuke them and bring them into captivity.

Whatever you allow your mind to dwell on will determine any changes in your attitude. Recognize My thoughts of purity, wholesomeness, joy, positive upbuilding thoughts and dwell on them. Cast down vain imaginations. My word says not to think of yourself more highly than you are.

Do not lie to yourself, for that is deception at work. Recognize where you are at and do not allow thoughts of pride or thinking greater of yourself to even enter your mind. Purify your mind. I love you, rest in that love.

JUNE 13

Daily Reading: 1 Samuel 16:1-13

Psalm 139:23,24   *Search me, O God, and know my heart: try me, and know my thoughts: And see if there be any wicked way in me, and lead me in the way everlasting.*

I cannot and will not give My glory to another. I the Lord look on the heart and judge its motives. Sometimes you do not even know your own heart with its motives, but I will reveal them to you. Nothing must be done out of vanity or self-glory, but because of your love for Me and the love you have for your brothers and sisters in Me. The very thing in other people that turns you off is the very thing in you that turns them off.

You must all be fellow labourers together, for one is not above the other. I have called you to serve and minister to Me, but not to be above others in the family of believers.

JUNE 14

Daily Reading: Genesis 32

Psalm, 34:7   *The angel of the Lord encampeth round about them that fear Him, and delivereth them.*

Praise, honour and glory belong to Me, and yet so often people would desire it for themselves. My word declares that My glory I will not give to another.

I desire your love and obedience. Stay close to Me and you will not find it difficult to follow Me. I will make your way plain and I will remove the obstacles. When you walk with Me, you do not walk alone. I am there beside you, in front of you and behind you. My presence will be all around you and I will give My angels charge to watch over you.

Remember Me this day. Think upon Me and My words. Spend time communing with Me, for I desire your fellowship. I love you.

JUNE 15

Daily Reading: Psalm 107

Psalm 107:8   *Oh that men would praise the Lord for His goodness, and for His wonderful works to the children of men!*

Praise Me for my goodness. I am blessing my people continually. You have read where My people Israel continually forsook Me and how I still had mercy and forgave them. I will have mercy even now, but I desire a people who would praise and bless Me from the heart for who I am. I desire to be loved by My people. I desire a love relationship with all My people.

Put your hand in Mine. I will lovingly watch over you. I will do things for you that no one else can do for you, or that you can do for yourself. I love you, you are My joy and delight. Have a good day in Me.

JUNE 16

Daily Reading: Matthew 8:5-13

John 16:24 *Hitherto have ye asked nothing in My name: ask, and ye hall receive, that your joy may be full.*

I am pleased that you are thankful this day. I am happy for you because you are excited. When you weep, I weep, but when you rejoice, I rejoice. Continue to praise Me and to rejoice in Me and this will be a day of blessing for you.

I have so much to give to My people, but their vision is too small. Look to Me, there is no end to My supply and to My giving. Enlarge your vision. You have set limits to what I can do but I have no limits. I desire to give freely just ask of Me. Look to Me as your God, your supplier. Place your expectation in Me and I will meet it. I will minister and I will rejoice over you today.

JUNE 17

Daily Reading: Psalm 90

Psalm 90:12 *So teach us to number our days, that we may applyour hearts unto wisdom.*

This is My day; rejoice in Me. I am pleased and happy that you came to spend time with Me. I desire your presence continually. So many of My people only come to me when they want something, which I do want to give to them; but first of all I desire your presence because you love Me.

Seek My face and My will. My will is to do the will of My Father and your will should be to do My will. Rejoice in Me.

JUNE 18

Daily Reading: Psalm 150

> *Psalm 115;17, 18   The dead praise not the Lord, neither any that go down*
> *into silence. But we will bless the Lord from this time forth*
> *and for evermore. Praise the Lord.*

Praise Me, praise Me much. Lift your eyes above everything else and praise Me. Praise Me for everything. Praise Me for your family. Praise Me in your heart. Praise Me in the sanctuary. Praise Me with other believers. Praise Me for the way I am at work in your lives. Praise Me for your children and how I am at work in their lives.

My word declares let everything that hath breath praise Me. That is true, but only man needs to be reminded to praise Me. I will bless this day for you, just let your praises come before Me.

JUNE 19

Daily Reading: Colossians 3

> *1 John 3:3   And every man that hath this hope in Him purifieth*
> *himself, even as He is pure.*

In My word you will find all the answers to all the problems and questions you may have. I will show you My ways, but you must decide to walk in those ways. You must purpose to put one foot in front of the other. My strength and grace is there to help, but you must purpose in your heart to walk in My way.

You must put off the old man and put on the new. I cannot violate your free will. Sometimes you want Me to do things for you, that you can do for yourself.

To receive My blessings there first is a desire in your heart and then there is a purposing in your mind and will. I am there to constantly help you and encourage you. I am your goal, keep your eyes on Me.

JUNE 20

Daily Reading: 1 Samuel 24

1 Samuel 24:17   And he (Saul) said to David, Thou art more righteous than I: for thou hast rewarded me good, whereas I have rewarded thee evil.

My child, I love you. I desire right heart attitudes for My people and for you. People will not hear what you are saying if your heart attitude is not right. They will only pick up on the attitude. My heart attitude is always right and pure.

I have no selfish motives. My motives are only to bless you and to help you. I desire the best for you just as you must desire the best for others. When you put Me first in everything, your heart will become right.

JUNE 21

Daily Reading: Proverbs 4

Deut. 5: 16   Honour thy father and thy mother, as the Lord thy God hath commanded thee: that thy days may be prolonged, and that it may go well with thee, in the land which the Lord thy God giveth thee.

Proverbs 20:7   The just man walketh in his integrity: his children are blessed after him.

Be a blessing to your parents this day. Love and honour them. In the same way you treat your parents, you will be treated. I know you love and respect your parents and I am pleased in that. You have had a godly heritage and there have been many blessings in your life because of it. Others have not been so blessed. Love them in spite of it.

You have had My hand of blessing on your life from the beginning. Praise Me for it and do not take it for granted. I love your parents, I love you, and I love your children. You have reaped many blessings because your parents and grandparents loved Me. My blessings will continue to your children as you faithfully love and serve Me.

JUNE 22

Daily Reading: Ruth 1:6-18,2:1-16

Ruth 2:12   *The Lord recompense thy work, and a full reward be given*
                   thee of the Lord God of Israel, under whose wings thou all
                   come to trust.

I love you My son, My daughter and I am pleased with you. I desire My people to be a blessing to others all the time. When you are a blessing, you bring glory to My name.

I will minister to you this day. I love you. I do not just say it, but I truly do love you. I gave everything for you. All that is mine is available to you. I desire to minister and work on behalf of My children.

There is joy in My heart when My children calion Me and depend on Me to work in their lives. You enjoy doing things for your children. I am your heavenly Father and I take pleasure in ministering to My children.

JUNE 23

Daily Reading: Proverbs 25

Proverbs 25:4   *Take away the dross from the silver, and there shall come*
                   forth a vessel for the finer.

You are special to Me. I am at work in your life. You need more discernment and wisdom in your life. I am enlarging your heart and soul to receive more of Me. Use discernment when sharing. Remember your fight is not with flesh and blood, and spirits will cause people to react when they are recognized.

As silver is purified the dross is removed; I am removing the dross in your life. You are My child. Depend much on My Holy Spirit to lead and guide you and to give you much discernment.

JUNE 24

Daily Reading: Isaiah 54

Isaiah 54:2   *Enlarge the place of thy tent, and let them stretch forth the curtains of thine habitations: spare not, lengthen thy cords, and strengthen thy stakes:*

I love you. I am continually strengthening you and enlarging your walls, so more of Me can be seen and be in you. I am showing and leading you in My ways. I will minister My direction to you.

There is unrest in your soul that is not from Me, and there is a cloud of confusion hanging over you. Rebuke the confusion in My name for the cloud of confusion is darkening your eyes. When the cloud is gone you will see My sun shining brightly. I am shining on you now, but the cloud is blocking your vision. Remember I have not moved, but the cloud has moved into a position so that it is blocking the sun.

Do what I have called you to do to the best of your ability. I will bless you for it. I am with you this day.

JUNE 25

Daily Reading: 2 John

John 15:7   *If ye abide in Me, and My words abide in you, ye shall ask what ye will, and it shall be done unto you.*

I love you, I have cleansed you, I have forgiven you and I have set you free. Now you must walk in the way I have called you to walk. Let Me, not desires rule your walk.

Seek My face continually. I am there ready to help, ready to listen and ready to meet your every need. Man has had a hard time understanding this, yet I love you so much. I desire a close communion with you.

Keep your eyes on Me at all times and the things of this earth will grow dim and won't seem as important. They will then take their rightful place, behind Me. Go in My peace and joy this day. I desire to give you a good day.

JUNE 26

Daily Reading: 1 Samuel 10:1-16

Proverbs 1:23   *Tum you at My reproof: behold, I will pour out My Spirit*
                     unto you, I will make known My words unto you.

I love you, that is an unchanging fact. I will be with you and minister My thoughts to you. I am your wisdom and all knowledge and I know what you need to hear.

Put Me first in your life. The television or books or other things must not take priority and become first in your life. Spending time with Me will change you for the more time you spend with Me the more you will change into My image. Does not My word say, "a man is known by the company he keeps"?

Rejoice in Me this day. Declare My goodness and My faithfulness.

JUNE 27

Daily Reading: Job 38

Isaiah 11:2   *And the Spirit of the Lord shall rest upon him, the spirit*
                     of wisdom, and understanding, the spirit of counsel and
                     might, the spirit of knowledge and of the fear of the Lord.

Every detail of life is planned by Me, right down to the veins that run through a leaf or a blade of grass. Your finite mind cannot comprehend My infinite mind. In Me you will find all wisdom and understanding, counsel and might and all knowledge and fear.

Ask Me for wisdom and understanding. Seek Me for counsel and might. Find My knowledge and fear. To everyone who seeks, the door will be opened. I delight to give treasures to My children, out of My unlimited storehouse. I love My creation, of which you are a part.

JUNE 28

Daily Reading: Luke 17:1-10

Luke 17:1   *Then said He unto the disciples, It is impossible but that offences will come: but woe unto him, through whom they come!*

I love you My son, My daughter, but when you say you love Me you must also obey My word. I have asked you to lay down the situation where your brother has offended you, and yet you talk about it and think about it. That is not obeying or loving Me. My strength and My power is available, but you must purpose in your heart not to talk about it any more. When you talk about it you are looking for people to lift you up. By agreeing with you, you force them to take sides and they will speak negatively of your brother. I do not do that. It is the work of the enemy.

You are all members of My body and I love you all equally, I will heal the breach between you and your brother and I will strengthen you this day.

JUNE 29

Daily Reading: 1 Samuel 30: 1-25

1 Samuel 30:6   *And David was greatly distressed; for the people spake of stoning him, because the soul of all the people was grieved, every man for his sons and for his daughter: but David encouraged himself in the Lord his God.*

You are finally coming to rest in Me. I received "your rights" when you laid down the control of your life and in particular the situation you are now going through. To come into rest, you must let Me work out the circumstances in your life and the direction for your life. I joyfully took "your rights" and made them Mine. I forgave and set you free from all anger and hurts.

Minister My love and understanding to those who have hurt you. They have fears and insecurities in their lives, fears that people will not accept them. Do not be discouraged, I will bless you and minister to you and through you. This situation has not been in vain; I will use you to strengthen the brethren. Rejoice and rest in Me this day. I love you!

JUNE 30

Daily Reading: Philippians 4:10-23

Philippians 4:19   But my God shall supply all your need according to His riches in glory by Christ Jesus.

My child, I love you. Let go of any preconceived ideas and of all feelings of rejection and hurt for they are feelings only, I have met your needs and I am looking after you. I will heal all the breaches.

There is a glorious hope and future awaiting you. So rejoice in Me. I will bless you mightily for My hand is upon you for good. I will bless this day and I will minister to your heart.

JULY 1

Daily Reading: Genesis 1

Psalm 8:3,4   *"When I consider Thy heavens, the work of Thy fingers, the moon and the stars, which Thou hast ordained; "What is man, that Thou art mindful of him? And the son of man, that Thou visitest him?*

Enjoy My beauty this day. I love it when My people rejoice in My handiwork. I have placed much beauty in My creation and I have made your country beautiful. 1created this world for you to enjoy and to take pleasure in it.

I am greater than the mountains. I am more majestic and I have more grandeur. As hard as it is to imagine, they can be shaken and moved but I cannot be moved for "I AM", that is My name.

This day see Me as your Creator, the creator of heaven and earth and all that is therein. I love you. You are part of My creation.

JULY 2

Daily Reading: 1 Timothy 4:7-16

Mark 6:31   *And He said unto them, Come ye yourselves apart into a desert place, and rest awhile: for there were many coming and going, and they had no leisure so much as to eat.*

I love you. I am glad you did not give way to the impulse to go shopping first. I have given you this time apart, this vacation, but I was waiting for you to spend time with Me first. I love you and I have cleansed you whiter than snow. Meditate on Me, My words and My works.

I am pleased that on this vacation you are discipling yourselves to seek My presence. I do not take vacations, I am always with you. There is so much I want to show and teach you both. I desire yielded vessels before Me, that are empty of self. I want the world to see what I can do through yielded people, those that love and serve Me. Give yourselves wholeheartedly to Me; and I will bless this vacation.

JULY 3

Daily Reading: James 1

Gal. 5: 16,17   *This I say then, Walk in the Spirit, and ye shall not fulfill the lust of the flesh. For the flesh lusteth against the Spirit, and the Spirit against the flesh: and these are contrary the one to the other: so that ye cannot do the things that ye would.*

There is a warfare going on. Your spirit desires to be close to Me but your flesh and your soul desire their own thing, They desire for feelings to be satisfied. When you obey Me your feelings will be satisfied and it will be a good feeling. When you give in to fleshly desires it will only satisfy for the moment, it is not a lasting feeling and it will bring guilt and condemnation. Desire Me and the feeling of contentment that I can give you.

Stay close to Me and be obedient to Me. Seek Me in every instance and obey My promptings. I love you.

JULY 4

Daily Reading: Joshua 18:1-10

Joshua 18:3   *And Joshua said unto the children of Israel, How long are ye slack to go to possess the land, which the Lord God of your fathers hath given you?*

My son, My daughter, I love you. Your life is hid in Me. As you advance in My kingdom, opposition will come. You were under attack, but I have delivered you.

Continue to press into Me. My word declares the violent taketh by force. Nothing will hinder you or stand in your way. You will with determination press forward. In Me you live and move and have your being. My Spirit is breaking through the darkness and My army will be victorious. March on. Every word that I have declared to you shall come to pass. Rejoice and be exceedingly glad.

JULY 5

Daily Reading: Psalm 31

Psalm 31:19,20   Oh how great is Thy goodness, which Thou hast laid up for them that fear Thee; which Thou hast wrought for them that trust in Thee before the sons of men! Thou shalt hide them in the secret of Thy presence from the pride of man: Thou shalt keep them secretly in apavilion from the strife of tongues.

My son, My daughter, I am with you and I love you. I desire for you to walk in total victory, but you are only walking in a measure of victory. You are approaching people and situations defensively and that is not walking in victory. Nothing will happen without Me allowing it.

Man can make all kinds of plans, but I remain in charge of your lives. You are where I want you to be. Be submissive, be teachable and love the brethren. Keep your eyes focused on Me and you will not be led astray.

Do not let any negative or defensive thought minister to you. Dwell on Me and My Word, confess My Word and feed on My Word. I am your defense. Your life is hid in Me.

JULY 6

Daily Reading: Psalm 34

Psalm 34:8   O taste and see that the Lord is good: blessed is the man that trusteth in Him.

My son, My daughter, I love you and I take much pleasure in the time you spend with Me. My ways have opened up before you and as you obey and follow My word you will discover more about resting. I am doing the work and you can rest.

There is much that I want to share with each of you. I have treasures untold waiting to be tapped into. Do not take the things I share with you lightly for they come from My heart to yours. They will bring great release and victory in your life. As you gaze on Me you will become like Me. Have a good day today My children.

JULY 7

Daily Reading: Psalm 46

Psalm 46:10   *Be still, and know that I am God: I will be exalted among the heathen, I will be exalted in the earth.*

Be encouraged this day. I love you and I will be with you. I will speak through you and minister to you. You have need to seek My quietness more often and I will minister to you in that quiet time. Quietness means shutting off the television and anything else that would disturb your mind, even the day's happenings; yes, even messages you may have heard.

Take walks with Me and let Me show you My beauty and let Me show you My wisdom. When a problem perplexes you My word of revelation will bring light to it and it will no longer perplex you. Read My Word more. Meditate on My words and let them take deep roots.

JULY 8

Daily Reading: John 1:1-18

Matt. 5:14a, 16   *Ye are the light of the world. Let your light so shine before nun, that they may see your good works, and glorify your Father which is in heaven.*

My child, I love you. I have called you to be a light that is pleasing to Me. I am at work in your life. Sometimes it will not seem that way to you, but you must believe it by faith. I am doing a good work in you. My will is being accomplished and you will be that light.

When planting a garden, by faith you believe you will reap a harvest after you plant the seeds. I have begun a good work in you and it will be completed You will walk in My kingdom principles so do not lose faith and hope in Me to bring it to pass. Praise Me for this and rejoice in Me this day.

JULY 9

Daily Reading: Exodus 25:1-8,36:3-7

Exodus 25:1,2   *And the Lord spake unto Moses, saying, speak unto the children of Israel, that they bring Me an offering: of every man that giveth it willingly with his heart ye shall take My offering.*

You are feeling burdened down by these requests for money. I love you, My child. My desire is not to take from you but to give to you and to bless you. I have shown you how to give and you have been obedient and I will bless you for that.

Feelings of pressure are not from Me. Men minister these feelings by looking to people to meet their needs, rather than looking to Me to meet their needs. This will place a burden of expectation on the people receiving these requests. There was excitement and joy in your heart when I enabled you to give. When you look to people to meet your needs, rather than trusting Me, you transfer a burden of expectation that should be on Me, to them. This burden is not of Me.

When I ask of you, I will also provide the means for you to give. This way it will not be a burden. My word declares My burden is easy and My yoke is light. My people must continue to learn this over and over.

JULY 10

Daily Reading: Numbers 22: 1-13

Numbers 22:32   *And the angel of the Lord said unto him, Wherefore hast thou smitten thine ass these three times? Behold, I went out to withstand thee, because thy way is perverse before Me:*

My son, My daughter, I love you and I desire for you to draw close to Me and I desire that you seek Me more and more. Spend more time with Me and listen to My voice as I speak. There are many voices speaking in the world this day, but I desire above all else, for you to seek out My voice to listen to.

There is much sin and corruption in the world, but in My presence is peace, holiness, pureness of heart and only one voice. There is so much confusion in the world because there are so many voices. My word declares, "My sheep know My voice and the voice of another shepherd they will not follow." Learn to listen to My voice only!

JULY 11

Daily Reading: Luke 6:27-45

Micah 6:8   *He hath shewed thee, O man, what is good; and what doth*
                         the Lord require of thee, but to do justly,
                         and to love mercy, and to walk humbly with thy God?

My child, I love you. At one time you also loved judgment and did mercy. I have been at work in your life reversing that order. As you have allowed Me to work in your life, I have reversed that so you now love mercy and do justly. Never judge anyone. Only I can do that. Let My love flow through you because when you minister in judgment you reap judgment from the world and Satan.

Disobedience to My laws will allow Satan an open door in your life to bring destruction. Obey Me and seek My guidance and you will bear My fruit which is the fruit of the Spirit.

JULY 12

Daily Reading: John 3:1-21

John 3:21   *But he that doeth truth cometh to the light, that his deeds may be made manifest, that they are wrought in God.*

My child, I love you. Seek continually to live and walk in My light. The world is in darkness and because its deeds are evil it cannot abide in My light, for My light will reveal those deeds.

Strive to live and walk in My light. Walk and live as My Son lived. He never left the light. I have chosen you to walk in My light and to abide in Me and to bear much fruit.

Draw close to Me and I will be close to you. My light will then be there to shed light on the path before you, so you will not stumble or fall or walk into danger. Praise and rejoice in Me and in My light this day.

JULY 13

Daily Reading: Mark 3:6-12,5:25-34

Matthew 11:12   *And from the days of John the Baptist until now the kingdom of heaven suffereth violence, and the violent take it by force.*

My child, I love you and I will minister to you this day. This day is My gift to you. There is a mighty work of restoration going on in your life.

The enemy of your soul has robbed you many times because you did not recognize him or his tactics, and partly because you gave him legal rights to do so. Continue to press into Me. The closer you are in Me the less he can bother you. He hates Me and he will not abide in My presence.

In My presence is fullness of joy. My presence is ever with you. I will lead and guide you this day. Just rest in Me.

JULY 14

Daily Reading: Titus 3

Titus 3:5　　*Not by works of righteousness which we have done, but according to His mercy He saved us, by the washing of regeneration, and renewing of the Holy Ghost;*

My child, you are pleasing to Me. You desire to be pure before Me, and I see you pure and holy before Me. I have washed you whiter than snow. You may think the snow makes everything clean and beautiful, but actually it only covers the dirt for a time, I make you clean and beautiful from the inside out, and it will not melt and disappear. I will be seen in you.

Incubate more and more of My word. Love the brethren and radiate My love and peace. You are making a difference for light always dispels darkness. You can be My light this day.

JULY 15

Daily Reading: Luke 18:15-17, Psalm 131

Matthew 18:3　　*And said, Verily I say unto you, Except ye be converted, and become as little children, ye shall not enter into the kingdom of heaven.*

I love you, you are a child of Mine. I am your heavenly Father. I am your Lord and your God.

You can come to Me for anything just like a little child that has hurt his finger. All that child has to say is, "I hurt", and Daddy will try to take care of it. Sometimes all it needs is a kiss and other times that same child will just want to cuddle in daddy's arms. I am your heavenly Father, I am here when you have hurts or needs or when you need to be cuddled. Please come to Me and let me be your daddy.

JULY 16

Daily Reading: 2 Corinthians 5

2 Cor. 5: 18   *And all things are of God, who hath reconciled us to Himself by Jesus Christ, and hath given to us the ministry of reconciliation;*

My child, I love you. I rejoice in you. You are hurting because of the breach there is in My body. This breach has come about, because I have given each person a different temperament, and because there is so little understanding and tolerance for one another.

I am calling you to the ministry of reconciliation. My body must be able to reconcile one with another and come back into proper relationship with Me. I desire for each temperament to be controlled by My Spirit. This will bring a greater understanding and appreciation for the other person in the body.

My word declares if any man lacks wisdom, to seek Me and I will give it liberally without measure. I am placing My thoughts and wisdom regarding this in your mind. The result will be that My body will grow in unity and love.

JULY 17

Daily Reading: Isaiah 26: 1-12

Isaiah 26:12   *Lord, Thou wilt ordain peace for us: for Thou also hast wrought all our works in us.*

My child, I love you. There is much turmoil and unrest going on all around you, but those who keep their eyes on Me will have perfect peace. I am bringing order and unity. To recognize that order is needed, there will often first be chaos and unrest. I am building My body, the Church.

Occupy yourself with what I have called you to do. Promotion cometh from Me. Keep your eyes on Me and always be ready to be a channel to bless and love those that you meet. My Spirit will do the work if you are willing to be that channel. Be encouraged this day and encourage My body.

JULY 18

Daily Reading: 2 Samuel 12: 1-25

John 13:8   *Peter saith unto Him, Thou shalt never wash my feet. Jesus answered him, If I wash thee not, thou hast no pan with Me.*

My child, I love you. There is no sin that can stand between us, if you are truly sorry from your heart and ask Me for forgiveness and cleansing. First you must ask Me to forgive you. I gave My life to forgive you all your sin and then I will wash you clean. You need My cleansing as much as you need My forgiveness. When I have cleansed you, the enemy will have no more right to bring it up again.

My cleansing must be received. I gave it to you, but you must let Me wash you. Some people have a hard time with this. They ask Me for forgiveness and I forgive them but they are hesitant about accepting My cleansing. This gives the enemy an opportunity to torment them. I am doing a good thing in your life, receive My forgiveness and cleansing, and let Me make you whole.

JULY 19

Daily Reading: Exodus 32: 19-28, Numbers 17: 1-10

2 Cor. 10:18   *For not he that commendeth himself is approved, but whom the Lord commendeth.*

My son, I love you and I approve of you. You need to be set free from a constant desire of needing approval from man, from those in authority and those around you. It robs you of your ability to serve Me, because it keeps your eyes focused on people and it will become a snare to your soul. You will say things to impress people, but that is not what is in your heart.

I, the Lord, check the heart and the motives of your actions. The enemy can use it to give you the wrong kind of recognition. When your heart is motivated by a wrong spirit it will come forth out of your mouth for the wrong reason. Again I say, I approve of you. When you seek to please Me, then men will also be pleased.

JULY 20

Daily Reading: Ephesians 6:1-4, Deuteronomy 6:20-25

Exodus 20:12   *Honour thy father and thy mother: that thy days may be long upon the land which the Lord thy God giveth thee.*

My son, My daughter, I love you and your families. It is good that you love your parents and visit them. Your relationship with your parents will reflect back to your children. It is a good thing for children to honour their parents and to esteem them highly. Your marriage is an example to your children, creating a desire in their hearts to have a good and happy marriage.

I am leading your lives step by step. Share freely of My goodness in your lives. Continue to always be open to My changes. Remember the Israelites, when the cloud moved they moved, regardless of their age. Do not become set in your own ways but always have your heart and ears open to My voice. Have a good day!

JULY 21

Daily Reading: Luke 22:31-46

Luke 22:32   *But I have prayed for thee, that thy faith fail not: and when thou art converted; strengthen thy brethren.*

My child I rejoice in you because I love you. Continue to desire My will in your life. Look to Me this day. You have need to stay in My presence for the enemy would desire to sift you and put you down, but in Me you will have the victory. Press in to total obedience to My word.

I am doing a good thing in the lives of My people. My light is spreading. The darkness is being penetrated, so that it will never be dark again. Remain in My presence this day.

JULY 22

Daily Reading: Luke 7:11-16, Mark 1:40-45

Mark 6:34   *And Jesus, when He came out, saw much people, and was moved with compassion toward them, because they were as sheep not having a shepherd: and He began to teach them many things.*

My child, I love you. Release your emotions to Me. To give and release them to Me will mean to becoming completely vulnerable, but fear not, for then I can come in and bring healing. Emotions are not a sign of weakness, but of compassion and of love.

I wept because I loved. Satan has not wanted that kind of love revealed and so the world has said, "strong men do not cry". That kind oflove is the strongest love of all. The love that shows and releases itself through tears and crying will break the hardest of hearts, it will touch the feelings of infirmities.

The love and compassion that Jesus had when He walked this earth reached into every heart, and He moved My heart when He cried out to Me, His Father. He wept and agonized bitterly with many tears when He prayed for this world to be saved. Ask Me for that kind of love. It will turn the world upside down.

JULY 23

Daily Reading: 1 Corinthians 4:1-7

Romans 12:3   *For I say, through the grace given unto me, to every man that is among you, not to think of himself more highly than he ought to think; but to think soberly, according as God hath dealt to every man the measure of faith.*

My people I love you. Rest in Me for I am with each one of you. You have each sensed Me speaking different things to your hearts, but do not be confused for I needed to speak and minister to each one differently.

I am enlarging my body from within, not enlarging in numbers but stretching each one to contain more of Me. My grace and Spirit is at work. There is a time of learning with the mind and then there is a time of working these principles in your lives.

Rest in Me and learn to be quiet before Me. Place all your confidence in Me especially when the leading may be different from your comprehension. Just know, your God is in charge!

JULY 24

Daily Reading: Revelation 12

Revelation 12:11   *And they overcame him by the blood of the Lamb, and by the word of their testimony; and they loved not their lives unto the death.*

Hebrews 11:5b   *for before His translation He had this testimony, that He pleased God.*

My child, I love you. You have need to draw close to Me. Many things are coming your way and they will have an entrance into you, unless you stay close to Me.

Do not take up defenses for yourself, but let Me be your defence. I have always protected my own. All that really matters is that you love Me more than anything that is said or done against you. It is the enemy that is the accuser of the brethren. His accusations will serve no purpose if we do not react, so do not let him rob your soul. Put your mind on Me. Rejoice in Me this day.

JULY 25

Daily Reading: Psalm 56

Acts 8:22   *Repent therefore of this thy wickedness, and pray God, if*
                 perhaps the thought of thine heart may be forgiven thee.

My child, you have been listening to the voice of the enemy. He has had you looking backwards to the rejection ministered to you in the past. I do not reject you instead I have urged you to press forward in Me. Yes, they did reject you, that part is true, but I have not rejected you, but Satan would have you believe that.

I will bless your obedience. Satan would like to destroy you through negative thoughts. My thoughts towards you are only good and positive so guard your thoughts and do not think negatively towards those who have rejected you. Receive My love this day and rejoice in it.

JULY 26

Daily Reading: Genesis 41: 15-36

Amos 8:11   *Behold, the days come, saith the Lord God, that I will send*
                 a famine in the land, not a famine of bread, nor a thirst for
                 water, but of hearing the words of the Lord:

My child, I love you. I am happy and pleased that you desired to spend this time with Me. Your life is being led by Me as you keep yourself yoked to Me. Mighty inroads are being made in the enemy camp.

My light is breaking forth in this city. I will have a storehouse in this city. In order for there to be a storehouse you must have something to offer to those who have needs. I will fill this storehouse to overflowing. They will not need money to buy of Me, just a deep desire to let Me love them and meet their needs. They must be willing to give Me their heart. Man cannot meet man's need; only I can. Go in My presence this day.

JULY 27

Daily Reading: Acts 12: 1-17

Acts 12:12   And when he considered the thing, he came to the house of Mary the In other of John, whose surname was Mark; where many were gathered together praying.

I love My Church. I will honour the times that you come together for prayer. My ear is always attentive to your prayers. They do not go unnoticed for I am and I will answer your prayers. One puts a thousand to flight, but two ten thousand and three even more.

I am doing a work in this area. As you continue to seek Me and intercede for My people, I will hear and answer your prayers. Continue to pray in the harvest and continue to pray for My kingdom to come forth full in you and for My will to be accomplished through you. This is My will for you and for My body.

JULY 28

Daily Reading: Luke 19:1-10

2 Timothy 2:21   If a man therefore purge himself from these, he shall be a vessel unto honour, sanctified, and meet for the master's use, and prepared unto every good work.

My child, I love you. There are many impurities in your life. It is when they come to the surface that you can see them. They make you say, "yuck," like dirt floating on the water. Remember, that dirt can be removed and the water can be made clean and pure.

Pray for a desire to be made perfectly pure. Your impurities keep you from being close to your God and fellow believers. Dirt attracts dirt. Before the new growth of spring can come, the dirty mess left behind by winter must be cleaned up. I am at work in your life so do not hold back but let Me do a cleaning and fill those areas with newness.

JULY 29

Daily Reading: Luke 3

Luke 3:18   *And many other things in His exhortation preached He unto the people.*

My son, I am pleased with you and I love you. I am pleased that you speak forth My words as I give them to you. Continue to listen for My voice and pray for much discernment. Satan is always there trying to interject his thoughts into My thoughts.

Keep your eyes on Me and then you will know if it is Me who is ministering. When you listen to other voices besides Mine, your mind will become confused. Confusion is not of Me, therefore you will know it is not Me ministering. I will speak to your heart. Continue to praise Me much. I will be with you this day.

JULY 30

Daily Reading: Acts 16:6-15

Rev. 3:7b-8a   *These things saith He that is holy, He that is true, He that hath the key of David, He that openeth, and no man shutteth; and shutteth, and no man openeth; I know thy works: behold, I have set before thee an open door, and no man can shut it:*

My child you go too much by feeling. When you do not feel like something you go against it. It does not depend on your feelings. Put all your trust in Me for your trust should be in Me, not in feelings, situations, circumstances or people.

Only I can open doors. I open doors that no man can open and I shut doors no man can shut or open. Your life is in My hands. I have a wonderful plan for your life and much preparation has gone into it. My plan will be accomplished.

Trust Me with your life for I love you more than you could ever love yourself. I am going before you, your steps are ordered of Me. Serve Me with gladness this day.

JULY 31

Daily Reading: Exodus 17:8-13, Hebrews 10:38-39, 11:14-16

Hebrews 11:15   *And truly, if they had been mindful of that country from whence they came out, they might have had opportunity to have returned.*

My child I desire for you to go on. My army cannot retreat. To do so is a sign of defeat. I have gone before you and I have won the battle. All you have to do is follow.

When you retreat you go backwards and that is taking your eyes off Me and turning around and looking the other way. When I have opened doors for you to walk through, do not look back from where you have come, but continue to look to Me to lead you even further.

Support others in the body also, who are getting weary and are starting to look back. Lift them up in prayer. I have led you this far and the road leads on. Be encouraged this day. I love you.

AUGUST 1

Daily Reading: 1 Corinthians 12: 12-27

Ephesians 4:16   *From whom. the whole body fitly joined together and compacted by that which every joint supplieth, according to the effectual working in the measure of every part, maketh increase of the body unto the edifying of itself in love.*

You have a special part in My body. There are many parts and all the parts are needed to make My body complete. My prayer is that there will be unity in My body, and Christians everywhere will know that they are members of the same body. There can be no schism in My body but there must be forgiveness and healing. Can one part of the body feel superior over another part of the body, or reject part of its own body? You know that does not happen unless there is sickness in the body. The body's immunity system will then take over and come against the sick cells that are taking over. My people come against the sickness within the body but not against the body itself.

We fight not against flesh and blood, but against principalities and powers in high places. My blessing is upon those who truly recognize My body. I love My body and every part is special to Me.

AUGUST 2

Daily Reading: Isaiah 58

Isaiah 58:6   *Is not this the fast that I have chosen? To loose the bands of wickedness, to undo the heavy burdens, and to let the oppressed go free, and that ye break every yoke ?*

My son, My daughter, you are My beloved. You are a part of My bride. Precious to Me is My body. There are gratings and rubbings going on in My body. The enemy of your soul is at work sowing discord and disharmony. Keep your eyes on Me and you will be victorious.

Love the rest of the body and especially reach out to those that are hurting inside. To love will require action on your part for the enemy is trying to destroy part of My body through their hurts. Comfort them and bind up their wounds. Focus on Me, the healer, and not on the enemy, the destroyer. I will be with you this day.

AUGUST 3

Daily Reading: Psalm 26

Psalm 24:3,4a *Who shall ascend unto the hill of the Lord? Or who shall stand in His holy place? He that hath clean hands, and a pure heart.*

You are My beloved son and I love you. Seek not to know what others might think of you, but seek to please Me in all that you do. I love you very much. I desire to fill you with My wisdom and My knowledge.

I desire for each one in My body to learn of Me and become pure in heart, to see and acknowledge Me in every situation in their lives. Not to be easily aroused by circumstances, but to look to Me and see where I am in it. It is the pure in heart who will see Me. Your sin will separate you from Me. Oh My people, that you would keep your eyes heavenward towards Me and obey Me and not turn to one another. Strive to run the race well. Keep the eyes of your heart on Me the author and finisher of your faith. I have run the race and you can do it also.

AUGUST 4

Daily Reading: 1 Kings 19:1-18

Psalm 37:1,5 *Fret not thyself because of evil doers. Commit thy way unto the Lord; trust also in Him; and He shall bring it to pass.*

I love you and I see your hurt. Trust Me to work out all the problems and situations for running away has never been a solution to problems. Istand and face the situation. Do not let bitterness or negative thinking overwhelm you and rob you of your joy in Me. You will then start to feel sorry for yourself and become totally depressed. The enemy would love to see you depressed and he will fill your mind with these thoughts.

I saw the sacrifice that you made and I love you. I will meet your need. I will bring to pass that which I have spoken. I am your help and your salvation. You can rejoice in this and praise Me for it. I will be with you today.

AUGUST 5

Daily Reading: Philippians 1: 19-30

Proverbs 23:18   *For surely there is all end; and thine expectation shall not be cut off.*

I love you. Keep your eyes continually on Me. My word is the light before your feet. I will continue to show you My way, but you must keep your eyes on Me and My word and not on people and circumstances. Remember one day at a time is all I am asking you to walk.

Your expectations must be in Me. I am unfolding My plan in your lives. The enemy would want to prevent that from happening, but My word will prevail. If you do not keep your eyes on Me, on My Word, and take heed of the words I have spoken to you, confusion will set in. Rejoice much in Me this day.

AUGUST 6

Daily Reading: Daniel 5

Daniel 6:3   *Then this Daniel was preferred above the presidents and princes, because an excellent spirit was in him; and the lang thought to set hint over the whole realm.*

I rejoice in the fact that you are willing to take the time to minister in My name. Continue to seek Me and strive for excellence in your life for My standard is not the world's standard. Mine is much higher and it is motivated by love. I look at the heart first of all. It must be pure with no selfish motives attached to it.

I came only to do the will of My Father and to please Him. My child, when you seek to please Me, you please My Father also. I love you, be open to hearing My voice this day. Rejoice much in Me!

AUGUST 7

Daily Reading: Jeremiah 3:11-25

> Jeremiah 3:22   *Return, ye backsliding children, and I will heal your*
> *backslidings, Behold, we come unto thee; for thou art the*
> *Lord our God.*

My child I have been waiting for you to come back and seek Me out. I know that you knew I was with you, but you did not take the time you should have to spend with Me. I long and wait for you to seek Me out.

I forgive you; draw near to Me and I will draw close to you. Be encouraged this day. Yield each day afresh to Me and I will renew and strengthen you. When you rest from all your labours and rest in Me, then you will be able to enjoy the land. You will not just tolerate or endure where you are at but you will enjoy My blessings. With My peace, love, and joy comes true enjoyment. Rejoice in Me and in My presence this day.

AUGUST 8

Daily Reading: Jeremiah 29: 1-14

> Jeremiah 29:11   *For I know the thoughts that I think toward you, saith the*
> *Lord, thoughts of peace, and not of evil, to give you an*
> *expected end.*

My child you are precious to Me and I love you. I rejoice in you. Satan would desire to put you down and minister negative thoughts to you but I am pleased with you.

Thoughts from Me will always be positive and upbuilding and I will never accuse you or put you down. Encourage the brethren in this. If the thought coming to your mind is negative, brings confusion, attacks you or condemns you, it is not from Me. You can bring these thoughts into captivity. I have come to set you free and to put Satan and his helpers into bondage. He would want to do the reverse. Rejoice in what I am doing!

AUGUST 9

Daily Reading: Luke 6:1-11

1 Peter 1:22   *Seeing ye have purified your souls in obeying the truth through the Spirit unto unfeigned love of the brethren, see that ye love one another with a pure heart fervently.*

I love My children; if only My children would realize how much I love them. My love will make them whole. My love will heal their hurts. My love will make them feel wanted. The world rejects them, but I desire to draw them close.

It is so important that you who know My love show and tell it to others. That is the magnet that will draw them. In order for My kingdom to rule on this earth, My people must know love for My kingdom is ruled by perfect love. Just as darkness cannot tolerate light, so this world with its principalities and powers cannot abide in love.

Seek My love in every situation. Seek to minister My love in every situation.

AUGUST 10

Daily Reading: Mark 12:28-34

1 Timothy 1:5   *Now the end of the commandment is charity out of a pure heart, and of a good conscience, and of faith unfeigned:*

My child, I love you. I too need to be told by My people that they love Me. I have waited for years to hear that. Most people only fear Me and as a result, they have not gotten to know Me and have not discovered for themselves that I am a God of love.

Love motivates My every move and action. It was love that caused Me to send My Son Jesus. I love you so much. My very nature cannot condemn those whom I love.

The difference between the Old Testament and the New Testament is love. The Old Testament was ruled by laws but the New Testament is ruled by love. Love causes action. Love causes a desire to obey those same laws but the motive is different. I desire a love relationship. Love as I love.

AUGUST 11

Daily Reading: 1 John 3:13-24

1 John 2:5   *But whoso keepeth His word, in him verily is the love of God perfected: hereby know we that we are in Him.*

My child, I rejoice in your love for Me. In every situation you must ask, "How can love rule in this". That is the same as saying, "How would the Lord rule in this?", for do you not know, I am love.

The enemy hates love; he is consumed with hate. He can not understand love because there is no love in him. Perfect love casts out fear and perfect love operates in faith.

My word declares, "If you love Me, you will obey Me." In other words, if you love Me, you will love as I love. As you yield more and more to My control, then more of My love can flow unhindered through you to others. You will be able to love as I love. I love you, My child. Have a love filled day.

AUGUST 12

Daily Reading: Nehemiah 4

Psalm 16:8   *I have set the Lord always before me: because He is at my right hand, I shall not be moved.*

I love you both. I am at work in your lives. Continue to draw closer to Me and I will draw closer to you.

Keep your eyes focused on Me. It is so easy to look at the world and things happening around you. Even the things you hear and see can bring you into turmoil. I desire for you to place Me before your eyes and I will lead and guide you. Do not let negative remarks cause you to become upset.

Be assured that when I ask you to minister to someone the consequences are in My hands. You are only the vessels through which I move. I am responsible for the results. I bring healing and restoration. I love you, rejoice in Me this day.

AUGUST 13

Daily Reading: Ephesians 1:1-14

Psalm 62:5   *My soul, wait thou only upon God; for my expectation is from Him.*

I desire to bless you abundantly, but sometimes there is not a confident expectation of good that I desire to do this. You are not worthy because of self but you have become worthy because you have been washed clean by the blood of Jesus.

I desire blessing for your life, but My blessing is not conditional upon what you have done or not done. I am not like an earthly father whose approval came your way because of what you did. I do desire obedience, but you have My blessing and approval because you have been redeemed by the precious blood of Jesus. It is not a conditional love.

I love you. Be confident in expecting blessing in your life. Your hope is in Me and in My word. Do not look at the circumstances, but keep your eyes on Me. This day let Me be your hope and place all your confidence in Me and I will bless you.

AUGUST 14

Daily Reading: John 3:22-36

John 3:30   *He must increase, but I must decrease.*

I love you My child. Great blessings are in store for those who love and serve Me and you are a part of them. You must decrease and I must increase. Self must continually be put down. It cannot rule or reign. I am the King of Kings and I must reign completely, but those that I commission I also give authority and power to reign with Me.

Out of your own self you can do nothing, but when I empower and anoint you, you will be a mighty vessel. Your identity becomes My identity the more you are in Me. The more you become identified with Me the greater I will be in you.

Rejoice in the work I place before you to do. You do not do it to please man but to please Me. I will be pleased with you!

AUGUST 15

Daily Reading: Ecclesiastes 3:1-15

Ecclesiastes 3: 1   To everything there is a season, and a time to every
purpose under the heaven:

My people I love you. Come boldly before Me and enter into My courts with praise. I will grant you a time of refreshing and a time of renewing in your spirit. You believe My words but at times your reasonings cause you to doubt and you have a hard time to let Me have full control. Trust every moment, every second, of the day to Me. When you do that, you can relax and let Me have full control.

You cannot control the time elements. It is commendable that you want everything on time, but when you yield that to Me, there will be a time for everything. The disciples were sometimes frustrated because I stopped and helped people along the way, but that was part of My schedule. My Father had commissioned Me to do this. Listen to My voice, relax and let Me organize your time.

AUGUST 16

Daily Reading: Joel 2:12-32

Joe12:25   And I will restore to you the years that the locust hath
eaten, the cankerworm, and the caterpillar, and the
palmerwonn, my great army which I sent among you.

My people, I will bring restoration in your life. Many of you, for lack of understanding and for not really knowing Me and My nature, have not really understood that the enemy of your souls has been there to rob you. He robbed you of blessings that I intended for you. I am a loving heavenly Father and I reward My children with My blessings. You have been robbed many times, but in My goodness I kept you from seeing it. You would not have been able to handle the hurts.

I will restore. You will reclaim the blessings that were meant for you out of the hand of the enemy. Commit all things unto Me and in thankfulness proclaim My goodness. I love you with an everlasting love.

AUGUST 17

Daily Reading: 1 Peter 3:8-22

1 Peter 3:15   *But sanctify the Lord God in your hearts: and be ready always to give an answer to every man that asketh you a reason of the hope that is in you with meekness and fear.*

My son, My daughter, I love you. I am at work in your lives sending people to you. Do not hesitate, but freely minister to them. I am opening these doors for you. They are hungry for My word and I have given you this word, "the bread of life," to feed them with. Your gift will make room for you.

Do not let the enemy minister feelings of inferiority to you; just keep your heart and thoughts pure. Minister My love freely and let My compassion touch them. Seek Me and I will give you direction and the words to speak. Go in My name this day and rejoice before Me.

AUGUST 18

Daily Reading: 1 Kings 5

1 Kings 4:29   *And God gave Solomon wisdom and understanding exceeding much, and largeness of heart, even as the sand that is on the sea shore.*

My son and My daughter I love you. I will be with you this day. I am in all the business deals you are contemplating. You need to continue to seek Me in every situation, to rest in Me and be assured that I will hear and answer.

I am pleased that you spend your regular time with Me, but you have not come into a perfect balance. The things of this world preoccupy more time than the time spent in My presence. Rather than watching certain programs on the television, shut off the television and seek My face. There is so much that I yet desire to share with you.

I desire to enlarge your spirit so you will become more and more like Me. Every business endeavour should be placed in My hands. Do not limit your sight to your finances but to My unlimited storehouse of blessings for you. You are blessed and you are rich!

AUGUST 19

Daily Reading: Luke 1:5-25, 57-66

Luke 1:20   *And, behold, thou shalt be dumb, and not able to speak, until the day that these things shall be performed, because thou believest not My words, which shall be fulfilled in their season.*

My child, I love you very much. You are being led every step of the way. Sometimes you think that it is not going fast enough, but everything is happening according to My plan and timing. I am enlarging you.

Do not let negative thoughts and doubts rule you this day. My Church is being enlarged. I am at work in the congregation enlarging her from within and without. I am at work moving circumstances in place to do a work in your lives. Be obedient to what I place before you to do.

Spend time with Me and let My words go down in your innermost being. Go in My peace this day.

AUGUST 20

Daily Reading: Haggai 1

Haggai 1:9   *Ye looked for much, and, lo, it came to little: and when ye brought it home, I did blow upon it. Why? saith the Lord of hosts. Because of Mine house that is waste, and ye run every man unto his own house.*

My children, I am with you. I have spoken to you regarding your giving and when I speak there is always a reason. I the Lord look upon the heart. My Church must come to order. I have allowed the financial situation to exist because I desire to bring about My ordinances in the Church.

My people, must consider their ways. Their first fruits belong to Me. When there is total obedience, there can be a total blessing also. I can even stir up the people around you to bless you.

Seek ye first the kingdom of God and all these things will be added unto you. When you are obedient to My commandments, then I am bound by My word to honour My word and pour out My blessings upon you. My commands are not grievous, but instead they are the doors that will open My blessing unto you.

AUGUST 21

Daily Reading: Ezekiel 28: 1-19

Proverbs 16:18   *Pride goeth before destruction, and an haughty spirit before a fall.*

My child I am with you. I love you very much. Your mind is in turmoil because you are looking at the circumstances in your life rather than keeping your eyes on Me and believing my promises. You become so quickly upset. The enemy is at work to discourage you and you let him in.

Pride let him in the door. Pride is not of Me. To be thankful in Me is not pride but to feel you are handling everything well is pride rising to the surface. Man without Me can do nothing. Pride is one of the enemy's greatest tools. When he has used it effectively and caused you to fall, he will then minister discouragement your way.

Let your life be an expression of thankfulness to Me. I am at work doing great and mighty things.

AUGUST 22

Daily Reading: Psalm 124

Psalm 124:8   *Our help is in the name of the Lord, who made heaven and earth.*

My child, I love you and I am right beside you. Continue to seek Me much. Give Me pre-eminence in your life, all the time, especially when remarks come your way that would make you feel down. As soon as you look at a situation, or at people, you have put Me down. I am at work on your behalf. Keep your eyes continually focused on Me. Things may be happening around you, but by keeping your eyes on Me, you will have clear guidance.

Believe Me; great things are in store for you. I delight to protect you, guide and lead you, set you free, comfort you and love you. It is for these reasons and more that I came. I will be with you today.

AUGUST 23

Daily Reading: Romans 12

> *Romans 12:4*   *For as we have many members in one body, and all members have not the same office:*

My child, I will prompt your heart according to who and what I want you to pray for. Sometimes prayer becomes a rote because it is not instigated by Me. Do not let others burden you down with prayer requests, but seek My way in this.

I have given special ministries in prayer to My intercessors, that is their calling and gifting from Me. Recognize and honour the calling I have given them. Do not feel guilty or condemned because you do not have the same burden and desire for prayer as they have. I have given you different giftings and called you to a different ministry.

Every part of My body has a different function but it all must work

together to edify the whole body. Recognize the ministry given to My intercessors. They go before you in prayer.

AUGUST 24

Daily Reading: James 2: 1-13

> *2 Cor. 10:12*   *For we dare not make ourselves of the number, or compare ourselves with some that commend themselves: but they measuring themselves by themselves, and comparing themselves among themselves, are not wise.*

My child, I am doing a work in your heart. Your security is in Me and not in people's opinion of you. You want people to approve of you, but all that really matters is that I approve of you. Man's approval comes from man comparing others with himself. Does not My word say that this is foolishness.

A nice dress does not cleanse the filth that is on the body, it only hides it. Man's approval can hide the things that I want to clean up or deal with. I desire a pure vessel for My kingdom. A pure vessel will always be noticed. Only if I place it aside will it not be seen.

My child, do not let the enemy discourage you. I look inward and I am pleased. Rejoice in Me this day.

AUGUST 25

Daily Reading: Galatians 1

Acts 1:24   *And they prayed, and said, Thou, Lord, which knowest the hearts of all men, shew whether of these two thou hast chosen.*

My people I love you. I move people in positions. The enemy tries to do this by using man's opinion of someone or outward appearance, but I the Lord look on your heart.

Whatever you do, do it as unto Me. If you do it to please man, that will be your reward. Man will speak good of you and your self ego will grow, but if you do it to please Me, I will reward you and men cannot help, but notice it, but I will bless you. This way you will grow spiritually.

The natural man can only feed the natural man, but I feed your spirit and cause it to grow and blossom and produce fruit. I can see the roots that have gone down deep, which man cannot see with the visible eye. Deep strong roots will cause there to be good fruit that is visible to man's eye. Whatever you do this day, do it as unto Me.

AUGUST 26
Daily Reading: Philippians 1:1-11

Psalm 138:8   *The Lord will perfect that which concerneth me: Thy mercy,*
O Lord, endureth for ever: forsake not the works of Thine
own hands.

I delight to bless My children. Bring all things and all thoughts into subjection
to Me. Do not listen to the lies of the enemy. My word will bring peace to your
heart but Satan would bring confusion and torment

I love you and I desire to set you free from all anxieties for they rob you of
My peace and joy. I am bringing you into a place of rest and security. All your
imperfections I will make perfect. I do not focus on the imperfections, but I see
you complete and perfect. I love you; rest in Me this day.

AUGUST 27
Daily Reading: Romans 8:31-39

Jeremiah 31:3   *The Lord hath appeared of old unto me, saying, Yea, I*
have loved thee with an everlasting love: therefore with
lovingkindness have I drawn thee.

My child, I love you. You will have no problem sharing My love when My love
is established in you. You will be secure in My love and you will know your
place in Me. There may be many things you need to learn, but you will never
need to question My love for you. That is a fact. I have spoken it to your heart
and you have believed it. That is faith.

You can believe it because you have been loved in the natural and so you have
no question or doubt in your heart about it. Some people can not believe it by
faith because they have been rejected over and over and so they question and
doubt in their heart. I will assure them over and over till they too can believe
and trust Me. My love will go with you this day.

AUGUST 28

Daily Reading: Genesis 13:14-18, 14:14-24

Hebrews 11:1   *Now faith is the substance of things hoped for; the evidence of things not seen.*

When something has been a part of your life, it is easier to believe Me for more. When I speak something to you and it has not been a part of your life, unbelief, doubt, questions and reasonings can rob you of that faith.

When I speak to a poor man, who has never had anything in his whole life, that I will bless him with prosperity and riches, everything within him questions this. Unbelief sets in because he cannot even picture it. When I speak forth a promise you must believe it and be able to see it accomplished. Do not say, "how can it be" or, "how will God do it?" I said it and I will do it. I will be with you today and surround you with my love.

AUGUST 29

Daily Reading: 2 Kings 2:8-22

Mark 11:23   *For verily I say unto you, That whosoever shall say unto this mountain, Be thou removed, and be thou cast into the sea; and shall not doubt in his heart, but shall believe that those things which he saith shall come to pass; he shall have whatsoever he saith:*

You question why we do not see more mountains moved. The answer is in My Word. If you had faith as a mustard seed it would happen.

Some will speak it with their mouth, but in their heart they truly do not see that mountain or obstacle gone. They doubt, reason and question in their mind. They do not look to the bigness of their God, but they look to the limitations of their mind.

When I speak something to your heart, see it in your mind as a thing accomplished for faith is the evidence of things not seen. Great things can be accomplished if men would believe My words and not question them. This is why I have to start with small things in man's life, to build his confidence in Me.

When you hear My voice and see in your mind what I am saying and not allow any doubt to enter, then it is accomplished. I love you very much and I will bless this day for you.

AUGUST 30

Daily Reading: 2 Corinthians 4

> *2 Corinthians 4:6* *For God, who commanded the light to shine out of darkness, hath shined in our hearts, to give the light of the knowledge of the glory of God in the face of Jesus Christ.*

My son and daughter, I love you and I am continually with you. You are My lighthouse flashing and beckoning to the world. You warn people and show them My way, warning them of danger and pitfalls. Your light guides them through the storms they are going through.

Without the lighthouse many ships would perish on the rocks. For those at sea, the light beckons to them and welcomes them home. They can see the light a long way off and they know the light will guide them safely home.

Let your light so shine before them, that they may glorify Me. I am going before and behind you this day.

AUGUST 31

Daily Reading: John 14:8-21

John 14:9   *Jesus saith unto him, Have I been so long time with you,*
                     and yet hast thou not known Me, Philip? He that hath seen
                     Me hath seen the Father; and how sayest thou then, Shew
                     us the Father?

My child I desire for you to be like Me, to reflect Me. I love you, you belong to Me, you are My son. A child will reflect the parent in an earthly relationship; how much more should you reflect Me for I am your heavenly Father. I desire for all My children to reflect Me.

That which is of the earth must disappear and die and that which is of Me must live and grow. You cannot change anyone, not even yourself, it is only I that can do that. Rest in Me. Rest in the fact that I will do the changing, but I can only change what is yielded to Me.

Enjoy this day. Freely I give all things to you to enjoy.

SEPTEMBER 1

Daily Reading: Numbers 11:1-10

Luke 9:62   *And Jesus said unto him, No man, having put his hand to the plough, and looking back, is fit for the kingdom of God.*

My child, I am leading and guiding your life. I see the desire in your heart to go on with Me. I have granted you this desire and moved you to this place in Me.

I have severed the ties to your former place. People would pull you back because they believe you should be there. They are not allowing themselves the opportunity to find out what My will is in this move. They are praying with desire in their heart and when they meet you they minister that desire across to you. When they truly see that you acknowledge this move as My will for your lives, then they will have to let go of you.

Advance in My kingdom and do not look back for it will cause you to stumble and fall. I will be with you this day.

SEPTEMBER 2

Daily Reading: 2 Chronicles 36:14-23, Ezra 1:1-5

Habakkuk 2:3   *For the vision is yet for an appointed time, but at the end it shall speak, and not lie: though it tarry, wait for it; because it will surely come, it will not tarry.*

I am with you and I love you. As it was with the Israelites in captivity in Nehemiah's day so it is now. At the set time, the appointed time, the Israelites returned to their homeland and their captivity was over. At the set, appointed time the things I have spoken concerning your lives will come to pass.

I will not delay, but I will do it. I will have a strong work in your area. A people that will know their God and do exploits so rejoice in Me, praise Me, and give thanks to Me this day.

SEPTEMBER 3

Daily Reading: Psalm 30

Psalm 94:19   In the multitude of my thoughts within me Thy comforts delight my soul.

I am all wisdom. You are in My hands and I am leading and guiding you. You must will your thoughts on Me. Do not get caught up in dwelling on others or situations that you have no part in, but place your thoughts on Me. I am at work and My plan is being unfolded. Give yourself to Me and My plan for you and I will work out all the details.

I love you. My children are all precious to Me. I know you and I understand you. You are pleasing to Me. I will heal your hurts and the misunderstandings that have caused these hurts. The enemy of your soul has been the cause of much of this. Sing and rejoice before Me this day.

SEPTEMBER 4

Daily Reading: 1 Corinthians 5

2 Cor. 13:5   Examine yourselves, whether ye be in the faith; prove your own selves. Know ye not your own selves, how that Jesus Christ is in you, except ye be reprobates?

My son, My daughter, I love you. You have a sadness and hurt in your heart over what has happened in My body, and that is good. You are a part of My body and when one part suffers the whole body suffers.

It is good to examine yourself and see if there are areas in your life in which I need to set you free. I desire pure and holy vessels for My service. Never let the thought take root, that this sin wouldn't happen to Me. Commit yourself wholly to Me, spirit, soul and body and it will not happen to you. Righteousness is not achieved by only thinking about it, but by putting your whole trust in Me and looking to Me for all your needs and answers.

I desire a holy and a righteous people. The enemy has for too long had My people follow his ways and his counsel and wisdom. Seek to know nothing else except Jesus who was crucified for your sins. I will be with you today.

SEPTEMBER 5

Daily Reading: 1 Kings 3: 16-28

Psalm 145:8   *The Lord is gracious, and full of compassion; slow to anger, and of great mercy.*

I am working My tenderness and My compassion in your heart. I desire to remove all the critical and judgmental attitudes and expressions that are there. Without My tenderness and My compassion you cannot reach out and touch others. They will only put up walls of self-defense because they sense a word of judgement and condemnation coming their way.

My people in this world need tenderness and compassion along with My insight. Let Me minister My revelation to you first and then I can use you to speak that with My tenderness and compassion. I love you very much. My heart is filled with compassion and mercy for you.

SEPTEMBER 6

Daily Reading: Psalm 51

Psalm 51:10   *Create in me a clean heart, O God; and renew a right spirit within me.*

You are My beloved. I am pleased that you apologized for your actions. I will make everything well. I shall give you favour with men and they will see Me in you. I have cleansed you from all unrighteousness and made you whiter than snow.

You have gotten wrapped up with so many other things that rob you of your time with Me. Seek Me and seek My face continually. When you keep Me before you continually, none of the other things will even seem important any more. I have forgiven you all your sins. Let My peace reign in your heart this day. I am going before you; just follow Me.

SEPTEMBER 7

Daily Reading: 1 Samuel 7:1-13

Ephesians 6:12 *For we wrestle not against flesh and blood, but against principalities, against powers, against the rulers of the darkness of this world, against spiritual wickedness in high places.*

I desire to set the captives free, but you must seek Me and ask Me to do it. Do not relax, but prepare your heart before Me. Before the Israelites went into battle they came and confessed their sins, prepared their hearts and sought My face. They fasted before Me. As they met before Me, I met their needs. When you do not seek Me it is too easy for you to rely on yourself and yet self has nothing. Only I can change things.

I desire to win the battle. When you seek Me for help you will also thank Me when I send help your way. Praise Me for the victory!

SEPTEMBER 8

Daily Reading: Isaiah 35

1 Corinthians 2:9 *But as it is written, Eye hath not seen, nor ear heard, neither have entered into the heart of man, the things which God hath prepared for them that love Him.*

My children I love you. My blessings to you are only the frosting on the cake. You cannot imagine how much of myself I desire to give to you. The world needs to see Me so much, but they can only see the measure that you allow Me to flow through you.

When you see people hurting, you want to take that hurt way but you cannot do that. I love My people in an even greater measure than you will ever be able to love and I can take away all the hurt, for I am Love. Every part of Me is love, hope, joy, peace and so much more.

I am restoring the bonds of unity and love within My Church. Every part of the bond that was broken" or crumbled will be made whole and it will be better than it was before. A mighty visitation of My Spirit is coming!

SEPTEMBER 9

Daily Reading: 1 Corinthians 3 :6-15, Deuteronomy 28: 1-8

Deut. 28:8   *The Lord shall command the blessing upon thee in thy storehouses, and in that thou settest thine hand unto; and He shall bless thee in the land which the Lord thy God giveth thee.*

I am pleased that you sought Me this day. Satan would desire to rob you of many things, even this day, but when you come to Me first, I will give the day back to you. Always seek Me first, You will notice when I bless you and the efforts of your hands, things will go so much quicker and easier.

Every task you do, whether great or small, if you do it as unto Me, I will bless and honour it and you will feel blessed that you have done it unto Me. Never look upon anything as insignificant or unimportant. To Me everything is of equal importance. I will bless the works of your hands this day.

SEPTEMBER 10

Daily Reading: Matthew 17: 1-13

James 2:23   *And the scripture was fulfilled which saith, Abraham believed God, and it was imputed unto him for righteousness: and he was called the Friend of God.*

My son I love these times together with you. My heart rejoices when you take the time to spend time with Me. Seek to spend more and more time with Me. Saturate yourself with My presence.

I desire to be your friend. I was Abraham's friend. He was not afraid to approach Me with his questions and I shared My heart with him. I told him what I was going to do. I desire this kind of relationship with My children. Before your children were fully grown you told them what to do. Now that they are grown up you share your heart with them for they have become your friends. I am knitting your heart to Mine. I love you!

SEPTEMBER 11

Daily Reading: Hebrews 3:7-19

Psalm 55:22   *Cast thy burden upon the Lord, and He shall sustain thee: He shall never suffer the righteous to be moved.*

My child, I love you. Rest in Me this day. Resting is committing all things to Me. When you have no burdens to carry, resting is easy. Burdens are not meant to be carried on your shoulders. I have said to My people to cast their cares and burdens on Me. The secret to entering into My rest is not to use man's ways, but My ways. The world's principles will not work, only My kingdom principles will work in My kingdom.

My promises are that you shall not want, but you shall rest in green pastures and drink from quiet waters. I will restore your soul and your emotions. You shall walk in MY righteousness with no fear of death or evil. I will provide food for you even when you are surrounded by enemies and I will comfort and correct you. I will give you My revelations, show you My ways, and pour out My blessings upon you.

SEPTEMBER 12

Daily Reading: 1 Samuel 15:1-26

1 Samuel 15:24   *And Saul said unto Samuel, I have sinned: for I have transgressed the commandment of the Lord, and thy words: because I feared the people, and obeyed their voice.*

You are affected many times by thoughts of how other people view and look at what you do. Sometimes you are more concerned about other people's opinions of you rather than Mine. You cannot be moved by people's opinions. This will bring bondages and snares in your life which will set you up for being hurt again. You should only be moved by obedience to My word, *logos* or *rhema*.

Your security and your confidence is in Me. Do not let other voices move you from hearing My voice. People may minister thoughts of guilt, anxiousness and trouble to your soul, but obedience to My word will bring blessing.

When you seek Me with all your heart, I will hear you and I will speak to you. I love you very much. Spend much time with Me today.

SEPTEMBER 13

Daily Reading: 2 Chronicles 14

> *2 Chron. 14:11*   *And Asa cried unto the Lord his God, and said, Lord, it is nothing with thee to help, whether with many, or with them that have no power: help us, o Lord our God; for we rest on Thee, and in Thy name we go against this multitude. O Lord, Thou art our God; let not man prevail against Thee.*

My child I love you and I will minister to your whole being. All your sins are forgiven and I will pour out My refreshing upon you. Everything will get done with time to spare so enter into My rest. Cast all your business upon Me, you can be too busy, but not feel that way or you may be accomplishing nothing and yet feel busy. The secret lies in trusting all your works to Me.

To trust Me is to totally rest in Me. To totally rest in Me is to completely trust Me in every situation. To trust Me is to commit everything to Me and not to lean on your own understanding or trying to figure everything out, but to relax and let Me work out all things in My timing, knowing I will do it. I speak rest to your soul this day.

SEPTEMBER 14

Daily Reading: 2 Peter 3: 1-10

> *2 Thess. 2:2*   *That ye be not soon shaken in mind, or be troubled, neither by spirit, nor by word, nor by letter as from us, as that the day of Christ is at hand.*

My child, I am with you and I love you very much. The enemy would try to overload your mind, but I am your covering, your protector. Put on My armour and the covering of My blood. I am at work changing you more and more into My likeness.

Cast aside all negative thoughts that the enemy would minister to your mind. Think upon My words, My promises to you and incubate them. Your thoughts must become filled with Me. Be ready to immediately put aside all other thoughts and replace them with My words.

You are learning this principle, but it must rule your life. Remind Me of the promises I have given you and thank Me for them. Speak back to Me the words of faith I have given you. I must do what I have said I would for I cannot lie. Let your thoughts rest in Me today for I am with you.

SEPTEMBER 15

Daily Reading: 2 Kings 5:20-27

Galatians 5:16   *This I say then, Walk in the Spirit, and ye shall not fulfil the lust of the flesh.*

My child, I love you and I desire your praises. I desire the praises of My people. There is much in the world today that is not pleasing to Me, it brings death and destruction to My people's lives.

To renew your mind daily you must concentrate on Me and My word. Keep your eyes focused on Me for what you gaze upon, you will become like.

More and more you are walking in My kingdom principles. You are putting on My characteristics and My nature. I am being seen in you. Walk in My ways today. Rejoice and be glad, for I am your Lord.

SEPTEMBER 16

Daily Reading: Proverbs 16

Proverbs 15:23   *A man hath joy by the answer of his mouth: and a word spoken in due season, how good is it!*

I am happy and pleased that you seek these moments with Me. Your strength for this day must come from Me. Daily you must seek Me. Be a light for Me this day and let Me speak through you. Do not talk just for the sake of talking, instead, praise Me.

You worry much about what people think of you and what you say. Do not be preoccupied with thoughts about self. All that really matters is that you please Me and that I am pleased in you. Share My love with those you come into contact with this day. I will give you a good day.

SEPTEMBER 17

Daily Reading: Romans 15: 1-14

Romans 15:5   *Now the God of patience and consolation grant you to be like-minded one toward another according to Christ Jesus.*

My people, I am reaching out to you this day for I love you. There are weaknesses in My body. It is because of having these weaknesses that you need the other person. I have designed it this way. Your weaknesses and failures will cause you to cry out to Me to help you and to be your strength in time of need.

Abraham, Jacob and David's weaknesses are listed so that you too can identify with them but I remember them not for their weaknesses, but for their faith in Me. In their spirit they never doubted My promises. Circumstances and failings caused them to take their eyes off Me and the promise I had given them, but they never denied Me or My promises.

Be encouraged, you have taken your eyes off Me many times and looked only on the circumstance, but then as soon as your eyes were on Me that hope was renewed. Love each one that comes your way for you need each other's weaknesses and strengths to be one.

SEPTEMBER 18

Daily Reading: Acts 7:17-36

Genesis 18:14a   *Is anything too hard for the Lord? At the time appointed I will return unto thee.*

My child, I love you, but you are allowing the enemy to bring you into turmoil. Rest in Me and rejoice that I am enlarging you. That which I have promised you will come to pass, but I have My timing. You do not like to hear about My timing for you feel it should be now. Rest in Me and trust in Me.

Do not place expectation on men. You do not like it when expectation is placed on you which you cannot fulfil. Remember man cannot open doors and move people into positions, only I can do that. Every step I move you into first is necessary in your life. You cannot see that now, but trust Me. Be faithful to what I have placed before you and I will open doors. I will minister this day to you, expect Me to move in a great way!

SEPTEMBER 19

Daily Reading: 1 Kings 17:10-24

Hebrews 13:2   *Be not forgetful to entertain strangers: for thereby some have entertained angels unawares.*

My son and My daughter, I love and care for you very much. You have need of Me this day. Do not let the things you have to do take pre-eminence over Me. I will be with you so all can be accomplished.

I am pleased that you opened your home, for being hospitable to strangers is commanded in My word. Do not worry about the provisions. I will provide and bless your finances. My desire is for you to be debt free. Blessings are in store for My people. My desire for you is not to be held accountable to the world because of debt, but to rule and be accountable to Me only.

I am bringing all of your life into My order. Let My peace rule in your heart this day.

SEPTEMBER 20

Daily Reading: Psalm 102:13-28

Isaiah 64:4 *For since the beginning of the world men have heard, nor perceived by the ear, neither hath the eye seen, O God, beside thee, what He hath prepared for him that waiteth for Him.*

My people, I love you. There is a glorious time coming for the Church. I will unfold My word and the things I have spoken will come to pass. Cast all your cares on Me for the battle is not yours, but Mine. I will take care of My people. I am calling you, as a body, to stand together. and see the salvation of your God.

My love is reaching out to My people. Instead of receiving My love, you react in fear. How much I would desire for you to know and understand My love. Stand and see Me fight the battle for you. You' will be amazed at what I will do, just rejoice and praise Me for the victory.

Every provision was made at Calvary and My hand is not shortened and My words will not return to me void. I AM.

SEPTEMBER 21

Daily Reading: 2 Timothy 1

Luke 12:4a *And I say unto you My friends,*

Proverbs 18:24 *A man that hath friends must show himself friendly: and there is a friend that sticketh closer than a brother.*

My dear children, I love you. My love for you cost Me My life. Your love for Me must cost you your life. Totally yield yourselves to Me and let your desires be My desires.

Work on spending time with Me as your friend. Friends desire each other's company because they enjoy sharing with each other. This day I would say you are My friends. I desire much fellowship with you.

Many things are going to happen in My body and in the world and I want to share them with you. My friend will you be there for Me? Will you spend time with Me? May I be your friend?

SEPTEMBER 22

Daily Reading: Luke 9:1-6,10:1-9

Revelation 3:8a　*I know thy works: behold, I have set before thee an open door, and no man can shut it:*

My child I love you and I am with you. I am causing the doors to open for you to minister just keep your eyes on Me. I am the one who must do the work. When you go in your own strength or in man's wisdom, nothing will happen or change, but as you seek My face, My annointing will be with you and upon you.

Many times in the past you have gone through difficult situations but that was so that you can now minister with My compassion and understanding. I love each one in My body equally. When I open doors and bring needs your way to minister to, it is because I have chosen you to be a vessel through which My annointing will flow. Thank Me for these opportunities.

SEPTEMBER 23

Daily Reading: 2 Corinthians 7

2 Corinthians 7:1　*Having therefore these promises, dearly beloved, let us cleanse ourselves from all filthiness of the flesh and spirit, perfecting holiness in the fear of God.*

My son, I love you and I give you My peace. You have allowed negative thought patterns to enter your mind, and the result is that it allowed the enemy to work a feeling of burden and heaviness upon your soul. You need to seek Me constantly as to what you should be involved in. I desire for the control of each day of your life.

Confess this sin of negative thought patterns to Me and let Me forgive and cleanse you. In the process you have ministered this burden to others. Cast all your care upon Me and I will take care of you.

You were looking at the many activities around you, but not at Me. I am not calling you to all these activities, so seek Me for discernment and I will show you My way. Keep your eyes on Me and then the activities that I call you to do will be a joy. Enjoy this day with Me.

SEPTEMBER 24

Daily Reading: Galatians 5: 1-13

Proverbs 6:2   *Thou art snared with the words of thy mouth, thou art taken with the words of thy mouth.*

My child, relax in Me. You are striving in your mind. You have been allowing Satan to minister a burden of expectation on you. You only have to abide and rest in Me. When everything begins to feel like a burden it is not from Me. I place burdens on My people that are easy because when you are yoked to Me, I carry the load.

Examine your motives at all times. If you plan things to get out of commitments and situations, that is taking it in your own hands. I place desires within you and then when you put Me first I meet those desires. When there is no desire to participate in something, don't look for excuses but recognize it could be My way of saying, you do not need to go. In Me you have a freedom to say *no*. My child I love you and I will be with you today.

SEPTEMBER 25

Daily Reading: 2 Peter 3: 10-18

James 1:5   *If any of you lack wisdom, let him ask of God, that giveth to all men liberally, and upbraideth not; and it shall be given him.*

My child, you have been taught to walk in wisdom. Use your liberty in Me, not to bring you into bondage, but to set you free. Insecurities and rejection will cause men to gather together because it is the only way they will feel acceptance. Immaturity in Me will do the same thing. Love the brethren and despise not their need for getting together . You do not have this need.

Walk in the wisdom that I have shown you. Let Me lead and direct your life. Recognize that a burden of heaviness is not My way of directing you. I shall minister My will to your desires and when your desire is to do My will you can then let those desires guide you. Have a good day, My child.

SEPTEMBER 26

Daily Reading: 1 Corinthians 7:1-16

Eccles. 4:9, 10a	*Two are better than one; because they have a good reward for their labour. For if they fall, the one will lift up his fellow:*
Proverbs 18:22	*Whoso findeth a wife findeth a good thing, and obtaineth favour of the Lord.*

My son and My daughter, I am with you. I have said that self must die. More dying to self takes place in marriage than anywhere else. Become vulnerable to each other.

Reach out to the partner who is hurting. Many times the hurting partner will not even realize that the other one is looking to him (or her) to meet his (or her) need, all he sees is his own need. He (or she) has established patterns in the years gone by, patterns of turning his (or her) thoughts inward and dwelling on self. This will not meet any need. It will only keep the mind occupied and rob him (or her) from truly finding release from situations and true inner peace.

Old patterns must be broken and new ones established. A true helpmeet will be willing to give all it takes to do this. Let Me bring wholeness into your marriage, two halves truly joined in heart, soul and spirit. Impossible? No with Me nothing is impossible. Ask Me and I will do it, says your God. Enjoy this day with the partner I have given you and together rejoice in Me.

SEPTEMBER 27

Daily Reading: Colossians 1:15-29

Colossians 1:18   *And He is the head of the body, the church: who is the beginning, the firstborn from the dead; that ill all things He might have the pre-eminence.*

My son, My daughter, I love you. I have begun a good work in you, but there is much more yet that I desire to do. You must become holy even as I am holy. There are areas in your life where the things of this world have taken pre-eminence.

Desire Me with all of your heart. The more you desire Me, the more the other will fall by the wayside. Determine in your will to walk in all My ways and I will be there to strengthen and guide you. Have a blessed day for I will be with you.

SEPTEMBER 28

Daily Reading: 2 Corinthians 2

2 Cor. 2:15   *For we are unto God a sweet savour of Christ, in them that are saved, and in them that perish:*

I am continually at work in your life. Your life will be like a sweet fragrance before Me. Keep your heart pure for out of it are the issues of life. Keep your mind pure because My word says as a man thinketh in his heart so he is.

My son, My daughter, strive for perfection and holiness. I am there to meet your every need, but you must call on Me and not rely on your own imagination or thinking. Though your sins be as scarlet, they shall be as white as snow. Though they be red as crimson, they shall be as wool. My blood washes everything clean and white.

I love you and I desire your purity, holiness and cleanliness before Me. The closer you live with Me, the more you will desire this. Be a sweet fragrance before Me this day.

SEPTEMBER 29

Daily Reading: Matthew 25:1-13

Matthew 7:23   *And then will I profess unto them, I never knew you: depart from Me, ye that work iniquity.*

I love you My child and I rejoice to call you that. There are many that think they are My children, but I do not even know them. To be My son or daughter I must know you and more importantly, you must know Me.

Spend time with Me and share your heart and soul with Me. Do not hide things from Me for I care for every aspect of your life and I am continually waiting for you to share everything with Me. There must be a close bond between us.

There will not fail one of the promises I have given to you for your life. When I have prepared you fully and I know I can trust you completely, they will be released in your life. To know Me is better than to serve Me.

SEPTEMBER 30

Daily Reading: Ezekiel 20: 10-26

Ezekiel 20:20   *And hallow My sabbaths; and they shall be a sign between Me and you, that ye may know that I am the Lord your God.*

My children, I love you. I have set aside this day for your rest and pleasure in Me. A day to seek My face and to worship Me with others in My body. Rejoice greatly over what I have done and what I am going to do. My glory will be revealed.

My people are beginning to hear My call. Great things are in store for My body. I rejoice that you take this time with Me. Wherever My people gather this day to worship Me, I will be there in the midst of them. Praise Me and praise My name for when you bless Me, I will bless you.

OCTOBER I

Daily Reading: Psalm 90

Psalm 118:24   *This is the day which the Lord hath made; we will rejoice and be glad in it.*

Psalm 71:18   *Now also when I all1old and grey headed, a God, forsake me not; until I have shewed Thy strength unto this generation, and Thy power to every one that is to come.*

I love you My child. Do not fear Me; I only desire the best for you. I place desires within you that I want to meet and fulfill. This is a special day to you and I desire a blessed and special day for you on your birthday. Each and every day is a special day for Me to remind you of your rebirth in Me.

I want to use you My child. Age is of no importance to Me for your life will continue to eternity. Continue to let your life be a vessel that I can use and flow through and you will be amazed at the mighty works I desire to do through you. You are My beloved.

OCTOBER 2

Daily Reading: 1 Corinthians 9:24-27,10:1-13

1 Cor. 9:27   *But I keep under my body, and bring it into subjection: lest that by any means, when I have preached to others, I myself should be a castaway.*

You must bring your body into subjection. Daily you must purpose in your heart that you rule your body, it should not rule you. When you feel like a drink and a snack, you go for it. That is not necessary. You have given in to feelings in this area and when you are listening to feelings you cannot hear My promptings.

You must walk in discipline. I will give you help in discipline, when you ask Me for it. At times it will be hard but I am there to help you, so bring your body into subjection and do not obey its every whim. Then you truly will feel better. I will be with you today.

OCTOBER 3

Daily Reading: Daniel 1

Psalm 16:3　　*But to the saints that are in the earth, and to the excellent, in whom is all my delight.*

Daniel6:3a　　*Then this Daniel was preferred above the presidents and princes, because an excellent spirit was in him;*

My son, I love you; you are blessed. Continue to set and keep your eyes on Me. Do not let the enemy hinder you in this for My hand is on you for your good. Set an example for those around you and cultivate an excellent spirit. Do what you do excellently.

Keep your motives pure. Ultimately you are not just pleasing men, but you are pleasing Me. Do not compromise My ways with the world's ways. My ways are higher than man's ways.

Do not question how will God do this or that, but rejoice because I will honour every word or command I have spoken. I will come through for you, rejoice in Me for this. I rejoice for the excellent spirit within you. Rejoice in Me today.

OCTOBER 4

Daily Reading: Malachi 2:11-17, Proverbs 5:15-23

Matthew 19:6　　*Wherefore they are no more twain, but one flesh. What therefore God hath joined together, let not man put asunder.*

My son, My daughter, you are precious to Me. I am pure and holy and I desire for My people to be pure and holy. I will bless your marriage. You can each love the other because you have both accepted and love the way I made you.

You have been willing to be changed by Me and the result is that then you are willing to change for each other also. You cannot fully grasp the principles of marriage until you submit yourself completely to Me. These same principles must be at work in My Church. You have learned this and I will continue to show you deeper truths. When there is no purity and holiness in marriage there is none in My Church. I love you both.

OCTOBER 5

Daily Reading: Genesis 17:1-22

Proverbs 31:30   *Favour is deceitful, and beauty is vain: but a woman that feareth the Lord, she shall be praised*

Genesis 17:16   *And I will bless her, and give thee a son also of her: yea, I will bless her, and she shall be a mother of nations; kings of people shall be of her.*

My daughter there is unrest in your soul. I love you. I loved Sarah as much as I loved Abraham and I love you as much as I love your husband. There is no need to feel inferior. You can rest securely in My love. I see you both as one. Without Sarah, Abraham could not have been the father of faith or the father of all believers.

I have placed you both together because you need the strengths of the other one to be complete in Me. Focus not on each other's weaknesses but on the fact that your strengths will cover each other's weaknesses. My word declares, "love covers a multitude of sins", and so your love for each other will cover a multitude of weaknesses. I love you and I will be with you this day.

OCTOBER 6

Daily Reading: Acts 2:1-4,14-21

Luke 4:18,19   *The Spirit of the Lord is upon me, because He hath anointed me to preach the gospel to the poor; He hath, sent me to heal the brokenhearted, to preach deliverance to the captives, and recovering of sight to the blind, to set at liberty them that are bruised, to preach the acceptable year of the Lord.*

My child, I love you. I rejoice in your praises to Me. My Spirit is being poured out in great measure. The world does not realize this, but My people will. I am calling My Church together. My power is displayed to bring people unto Me.

My body is very hurt. She has been abused and beaten and torn apart by the enemy. But I am raising up an army to bring relief, to bind up the wounds, to heal the brokenhearted, to teach My word and to set the captives free. You will be a part of this army.

Continue to keep your eyes on Me. At times My voice will speak softly, but if you remain close by My side you will not miss Me speaking to you. Encourage the hearts of the brethren this day. You are a part of My army!

OCTOBER 7

Daily Reading: Matthew 13:24-30, 36-43

3 John v.ll   *Beloved follow not that which is evil, but that which is good. He that doeth good is of God: but he that doeth evil hath not seen God.*

1 John 3:16   *Hereby perceive we the love of God, because He laid down His life for us: and we ought to lay down our lives for the brethren.*

My son, My daughter, I love you. I have called and molded and shaped you to be an important part in My body. My Church will know healing. I desire for My body to prosper and be in health. The day of reaction to one another is over and you must now come into maturity and flow with one another and minister to those in need. Children react to one another because they are immature. My body must grow up unto Me to be able to do what I do.

I am the head of the body. Many times My Church does not recognize Me as their head. They are doing what they want to do, not what I want them to do. I will go before you this day to lead and direct you. I am with you!

OCTOBER 8

Daily Reading: 2 Thessalonians 3, John 21:20-23

1 Peter 4:15   *But let none of you suffer as a murderer, or as a thief, or as an evil doer, or as a busybody in other men's matters.*

John 21:22   *Jesus saith unto him, If I will that he tarry till I come, what is that to thee? Follow thou Me.*

My child, I love you. You have many questions tumbling through your mind. Leave them all to Me. Be obedient to all that I have called and chosen you for. You are only accountable for what I have spoken to you. Do not become a busybody in other men's lives. They are accountable to Me for their doings. I lead and direct each person's life.

Enjoy this day and enjoy the fellowship with My people. Praise and worship Me this day. You have desires in your heart that I have placed there. They are My desires and My calling for YOU and they are not meant for someone else. I will bring this to pass in your life.

OCTOBER 9

Daily Reading: Proverbs 8

Luke 21:15   *For I will give you a mouth and wisdom, which all your adversaries shall not be able to gainsay nor resist.*

I love you, My child. I am pleased that you are spending this time with Me. I rejoice over you. I will answer your questions concerning yourself and I will continue to give you more wisdom and greater insight. This will help you to further understand yourself and others. I delight to answer your prayers.

There are many afflicted and held in chains by the enemy, but I desire to see them set free. I have given you the keys to unlock the chains, for all authority has been given to My Church. Use My authority. Freely you have received, freely give. I will bless you and keep you this day.

OCTOBER 10

Daily Reading: Jonah 3,4

Hosea 14:4   *I will heal their backsliding, I will love them freely: for Mine anger is turned away from him.*

You are My son, My daughter and My child. You would sacrifice of yourself to give to your children. That is how I am. My love for you is beyond human understanding, it reaches out to you constantly to make your burdens lighter and to show and give you direction.

You have been concerned for your children and even the anger or frustration you felt came because of your concern for their well being. I love you so much more than that. My anger is aroused when I see the enemy of your souls laying traps and ensnaring you, hurting you and even deceiving you into believing it is Me doing those things to My children. I do not do those things for I can only love.

Love Me this day and love one another fervently. Look at everything that happens in the light of My Word, to know whether or not it truly is of Me. I love you this day.

OCTOBER 11

Daily Reading: Ecclesiastes 5

Ecclesiastes 5: 19 Every man also to whom God hath given riches and wealth, and hath given him power to eat thereof, and to take his portion and to rejoice in his labour; this is the gift of God.

My child, I am with you. Continue to see and recognize My hand in everything. I love you very much. Riches are only one of the means that I can use to bless My children, but do not focus on riches, but rather on Me, the giver of all these blessings.

Be ready to share out of the abundance that I give you. When I give you treasures from My Word, be ready to share with others. Everything you have and all that you are, you have received from Me. To those who are responsible and accountable I give more. Blessed are you of the Lord, My child!

OCTOBER 12

Daily Reading: Malachi 3: 1-15

Proverbs 3:9, 10 Honour the Lord with thy substance, and with the firstfruits of all thine increase: So shall thy barns be filled with plenty and thy presses shall burst out with new wine.

My child, I love you. I rejoice over you. You are blessed. Continue to follow Me and My words for they will never lead you astray. Seek Me in every step of your life, even in your finances. I will lead and guide you. You will be amazed at what I am going to do. I will loosen finances in your favour and give you clear direction.

Doors are being opened for you and you will know that it is only Me that is able to open those doors. I am pouring out my blessings upon you and there will not be enough room to contain it all. Freely you have received, freely give. Remain in My peace and joy this day.

OCTOBER 13

Daily Reading: 1 Chronicles 14:8-17

Psalm 66:20   *Blessed be God, which hath not turned away my prayer, nor His mercy from, me.*

Prayer is communion with Me. Communion is a two way street. You need to hear as well as talk. Many in My body do not really understand this. They continually bring their problems to Me without ever hearing the answer or solution from Me. They do not stop and wait and listen for My voice to speak to them.

How I desire to communicate with My people. You need to continue to seek Me much for further communion and revelations. I will be with you this day. Bless Me this day. Draw nigh to Me and I will draw nigh to you.

OCTOBER 14

Daily Reading: Acts 20:6-12

Hebrews 10:25   *Not forsaking the assembling of ourselves together, as the manner of some is; but exhorting one another: and so much the more, as ye see the day approaching.*

My son, I love you. You are a valuable part of My body. I am opening more and more doors of service for you. Keep your eyes focused on Me and listen for My voice. I will be with you this day. I will bless the worship service, My love will minister effectively.

All the needs of the body are met by Me, but I need human vehicles through which I can minister. When you are not obeying My voice someone in My body cannot receive what I have for them. I have chosen to work through My body to edify, to comfort, to heal, to bring My word, and to rejoice. Place your eyes on Me this day.

OCTOBER 15

Daily Reading: Genesis 7

Genesis 7: 1, 16	*And the Lord said unto Noah, Come thou and all thy house into the ark; for thee have I seen righteous before Me in this generation. And they that went in, went in male and female of all flesh, as God had commanded him: and the Lord shut him in.*

My son and My daughter, I am with you. I love you both. When the storms are raging outside, you are safe in your house, and so it is with your life. When your life is hid in Me you are safe from all the storms and elements that come your way. Even now I have placed My angels around you to keep you all safe. No enemy can infiltrate My hedge of protection.

Keep yourselves pure, remain in Me and remain in My Word. Seek Me much and learn of Me. I am leading and guiding your lives. I will be with you this day,

OCTOBER 16

Daily Reading: Ezekiel 34: 1-10

Jeremiah 50:6	*My people hath been lost sheep: their shepherds have caused them to go astray, they have turned them away on the mountains: they have gone from mountain to hill, they have forgotten their resting place.*

My people, I love you. I will give you pastors who will show you My kingdom principles and not burden you down with more of the world's rules and traditions of men. These other shepherds have tried to enter My kingdom by works. They have left the mountains, the high places in Me and settled for the hills, the mediocre, the in-between.

In the natural, a hill is easier to climb than a mountain, but I have said I would give My people feet like hinds' feet to climb the high places. These animals can scale and climb, seemingly with no effort at all, the highest mountain and the steepest cliff. You do not need hinds' feet to climb the hills, man's ways can get you there. That is the secret to entering My rest, man's ways will not get you there.

OCTOBER 17

Daily Reading: Acts 15:1-21

Acts 15:9   *And put no difference between us and them, purifying their hearts by faith.*

You needed Me so much these past days, but you ignored Me a lot. So many times frictions came your way because you had not sought Me or My protection for the day. I will never leave you nor forsake you. When you do not seek Me or My help, you end up doing things on your own. You did not put Me or My armour on. When you put Me on, I can rule through you and protect you.

I love you and I have forgiven and cleansed you. You need Me so much. I desire for My people to love each other. This way, when the enemy is at work, you stand together rather than against each other.

I will be with you this day. Seek My nearness and remain in My presence.

OCTOBER 18

Daily Reading: Exodus 16:14-36

Psalm 143:8   *Cause me to hear Thy loving kindness in the morning; for in Thee do I trust: cause me to know the way wherein I should walk; for I lift up my soul unto Thee.*

My child, I have missed you. I love you very much. Never get too busy to spend time with Me. It is so easy to get caught up in the things of this world and the busyness of life, that you forget to spend time with Me. The time spent with Me will equip and strengthen you for the day.

I will grant you a refreshing that comes only early in the morning. It comes like the morning dew on the grass, as soon as the heat of the day comes it evaporates but the ground and the plants have absorbed the moisture and taken its benefits. Without the morning dew, the heat of the day could prove too much for the plants. So it is with you; it is that time in the morning when I will refresh you and it will keep you going all day. The heat of the day, pressures from within and without, will not affect you the same if you have had that time of refreshing with Me. I will bless you this day

OCTOBER 19

Daily Reading: Proverbs 7

> Proverbs 7:25   *Let not thine heart decline to her ways, go not astray in her paths.*

My child, I love you. I desire to minister to you this day. You are troubled but you do not need to be. Keep your eyes fixed singly on My word and My commandments. Yes, the enemy will come as an angel of light but there will always be untruth in what he has to say. The greatest men of God will be attacked the hardest.

Keep your heart pure by obeying My word and My commandments. Never suppose yourself to be above temptation for My word warns against pride, and I resist the proud. Only those who humbly come to Me will I show My ways and My words.

Know My Word and ask for My Spirit of revelation and wisdom to understand My Word. I will never go against My Word. I am a pure and holy God and I desire purity and holiness among My followers. When you put Me first in all of your ways, I will direct your paths.

OCTOBER 20

Daily Reading: 1 Thessalonians 2

> 1 Thess. 2:12   *That ye would walk worthy of God, who hath called you unto His kingdom and glory.*

My son and My daughter, I love you. I have heard your prayers. You are washed, you are cleansed, you are forgiven, you are restored, and you are being filled more and more with Me. Bring into captivity every thought that is not from Me. As you do this, not only will your mind be renewed, but you will be more pleasing to Me.

Press farther and farther into My kingdom to totally occupy My kingdom and to rule in My kingdom. Do not relax while pressing on for the enemy would lull you into a false sense of security. My children, I desire for you to enjoy My kingdom, to have rest from without. Deny fleshly desires, for My kingdom is not a fleshly kingdom. Press on in Me.

OCTOBER 21

Daily Reading: Philemon 1-25

Philemon v.16   Not now as a servant, but above a servant, a brother
beloved, specially to me, but how much more unto thee,
both in the flesh, and in the Lord?

My son, My daughter, I love you. You are My friends. I share My thoughts with you as with a friend. My Word declares that a servant knows not what the Lord doeth; but a friend does, because he shares His thoughts with Him. My Word also declares that a child does not differ from a servant when he is young, but when he grows up he becomes like a friend. He enters into sonship with its full responsibilities.

I desire to share My thoughts with you. I desire for you to share your thoughts with Me, not just a "hi and how are you." To be a true friend there must be a relationship of trust. Trusting each others' judgments and believing in each other. Trust My judgement for your life and believe in Me above all others for My desire for your life will always be the best. If you believe that, you will not question My ways. I will be with you today and I want to share My thoughts with you.

OCTOBER 22

Daily Reading: Acts 1:1-14

Jude v.20,21   But ye, beloved, building up yourselves on your most holy
faith, praying in the Holy Ghost, Keep yourselves in the
love of God, lookingfor the mercy of our Lord Jesus Christ
unto eternal life.

My child, you are learning to trust Me more and more. Continue to lay aside all reasonings of your mind. Come in faith, believing I will not lead you astray. With Me in control you do not need to fear the future. My child, I have only the best in store for you. Do not fear Me or My dealings. I will not hurt you, like people have hurt you. I only want to love you and make you more like Me.

Constantly keep your eyes on Me, the author and finisher of your faith. I am leading you day by day, one step at a time. Let Me be first in all your ways and thoughts and actions. I love you.

OCTOBER 23

Daily Reading: 1 Samuel 14:1-14

1 Samuel 14:6   *And Jonathan said to the young man that bare his armour,*
Come, and let us go over unto the garrison of these
uncircumcised: it may be that the Lord will work:for us: for
there is no restraint to the Lord to save by many or by few.

My child, I am right there beside you and I love you. I will strengthen you and uphold you. I will give you a spirit of wisdom and counsel. I will lead you and direct your ways, just be a channel through which I can flow. Do the work I have called you to do and enjoy what your hands find to do.

Cease striving in your own mind. There are many thoughts there that you should not even be thinking. I desire to give you a good day. Rejoice much in Me for that will cause negative thoughts to disappear. I will be with you this day.

OCTOBER 24

Daily Reading: Matthew 5:43-48,7:1-12

Matthew 7: 12   *Therefore all things whatsoever ye would that men should*
do to you, do ye even so to them: for this is the law and
the prophets.

My beloved people, I love you. Ask Me how you can help each other. Ask Me how you can love each other. Ask Me how you can bless each other. There will always be new ways to do these things. Emotional needs are just as important as physical needs. There must be a balance in spiritual, emotional and physical needs. When one area is neglected or not touched the other two areas will also show an imbalance.

Your walk with Me is affected when your walk with each other is not as it should be. The more you love each other the more you can love Me. The more you reach out to each other the more I reach out to you.

OCTOBER 25

Daily Reading: 2 Corinthians 8

*2 Cor. 8:16   But thanks be to God, which put the same earnest care
into the heart of Titus for you.*

My people, I love you. I care for and love My body very much. That care and
love can be seen in My servants for they are united with Me. Each one is a
member of My body, with Me as the head and you are a part of Me. When you
rest and let the head make the decisions you will automatically do what I would
do because you are not striving, but flowing with Me, your head. My Spirit is
there to help you.

Let Me lead you today and My love and care will flow through you to those who
are in need. My word declares that My goodness will lead men to repentance.
People need to feel and know My goodness in their life. Love them and they
will respond to you. I will be with you today.

OCTOBER 26

Daily Reading: Exodus 2:11-25

*Exodus 3:10   Come now therefore, and I will send thee unto Pharaoh,
that thou mayest bring forth My people the children of
Israel out of Egypt.*

There are many times that you are like a butterfly. First, you were a caterpillar
going where you wanted to go, but then I bound you up in a cocoon. I brought
that bondage in your life so that you were no longer free and you could only do
the things that I allowed you to do. It is a period of inactivity, of doing nothing
and yet wanting to be free. Then comes the day of emerging. No longer are you
bound. You are now a butterfly for Me. My beauty is there for all to see.

I will send you here and there. You will bring My fruit, My fragrance, My
beauty to those who see you. Do and be what I have called you to be. A son, a
daughter, in service for their King.

OCTOBER 27

Daily Reading: Philippians 2: 1-18

Acts 4:13   *Now when they saw the boldness of Peter and John, and perceived that they were unlearned and ignorant men, they marvelled; and they took knowledge of them, that they had been with Jesus.*

I see a desire for a pure heart, but with mixed motives. Your motives must not be for self, but only to please Me and be acceptable in My sight because you love Me so much. I love you that much. I am at work in your life, ever changing you into My likeness.

More and more as your heart is yielded to Me, I will change you and the world will see My likeness in you. My disciples were recognized because they had been with Me. Spend much time with Me for you belong to Me and in My kingdom.

Lose yourself in Me and let Me find you, let Me show you who you really are in Me. I see only what is pure and holy for I cannot look upon sin. You have been washed and cleansed by My blood. You have been redeemed and I am changing you from the inside out. Spend this day with Me in My presence.

OCTOBER 28

Daily Reading: 1 Corinthians 9: 15-27

Proverbs 4:26   *Ponder the path of thy feet, and let all thy ways be established.*

My child you are precious to Me and I love you. Walk continually in My ways and set them as goals before you. When you run a race you have a goal before you, that goal is the finish line, and the prize at the finish line. I have placed goals before you, the purpose for which you are called. You are called to be a part of My kingdom to show forth My praises, to be My representative in this world, Keep these goals before you. Satan would deter you, place roadblocks in your way, disable you or destroy you.

Only those that keep the faith will win. Look not to the right or to the left for that will sidetrack you, but keep your eyes on Me. I will strengthen and equip you for you do not walk alone. I go with you.

OCTOBER 29

Daily Reading: Amos 8

Amos 3:7   *Surely the Lord God will do nothing, but He revealeth His secret unto His servants the prophets.*

My child, I love you. I rejoice because you seek this time with Me. There is a famine in the land of hearing My word and My voice. Many are going to churches, but they do not know My voice. I have said in My word that I will speak and tell My prophets what I will do in the world before it happens. I have always done that. I told Abraham about the destruction of Sodom and Gomorrah. I showed Moses, Elijah, My disciples and many more of the things that were to come and I will do the same today. My disciples, My prophets and My people need to hear My voice today.

My child, these times together are very precious. Do not take them lightly, but seek Me continually. I love you and I will be with you this day.

OCTOBER 30

Daily Reading: Luke 11:1-13

Mark 11:24   *Therefore I say unto you, What things soever ye desire,*
when ye pray believe that ye receive them, and ye shall
have them.

My child, I love you. I have given you many blessings. You are just beginning to discover the many blessings I have poured out on you and your family.

Now it is the time to pick up the call to pray. My word and work will be superseded by prayer from My people. People united in Me and united in their goal and vision. Hear the call to pray! My heart rejoices when you respond to the call to pray. Many are called, but few are chosen. I have chosen you for this task.

OCTOBER 31

Daily Reading: Job 29

Job 29:14   *I put on righteousness, and it clothed me: my judgment*
was as a robe and a diadem.

My child I am with you. I love you and I desire for you to be constantly in My presence. Search out every cause. Bring every detail of your life to Me for I desire to show you My way in the very details of your life. I desire to go before you and to walk with you. Put on My righteousness and My armour.

My word will not return void. I have given you many promises and not one of them shall fail. Let Me work out all things in your lives. Do not try to figure things out for My ways are beyond human comprehension. Will you spend time in My presence today?

NOVEMBER 1

Daily Reading: Psalm 127

Proverbs 20:7   *The just man walketh in his integrity: his children are blessed after him.*

My daughter, I love you. Each one of My children are precious to Me just as each one of your children are precious to you. They are all different, yet you love them all equally. You desire to do things for them and to bless them when you can. That is what the heart of a parent is like. My heart is like that also.

There is so much I desire to give to you and to do for you. Keep Me first in all your plans. Tell Me everything that goes on in your life. I hear your prayers for your children and I am with your children. They have been blessed by Me. Have a good day today,

NOVEMBER 2

Daily Reading: 1 Chronicles 28

1 Chronicles 22:5   *And David said, Solomon my son is young and tender, and the house that is to be builded for the Lord must be exceeding magnifical, of fame and of glory throughout all countries: I will therefore now make preparation for it. So David prepared abundantly before his death.*

My son, I am walking beside you and our relationship is a love relationship. I desire for you to share your heart with Me and I desire to share My heart with you. I desire to bless you as you bless your children. You are there to help them in whatever way you can when you sense they need that help. That is the heart of a father speaking.

I have those same desires. I am your heavenly father and I want to pour out My blessings on you. You worry whether your children will accept your gift of help. Will you accept what I desire to do in your life, the blessings that I desire to give to you? Do not fear Me. I desire to clothe you in My beauty and holiness.

NOVEMBER 3

Daily Reading: 1 Kings 10: 1-13

1 Kings 10:6,7a   And she said to the king, It was a true report that I heard in mine own land of thy acts and of thy wisdom. Howbeit I believed not the words, until I came, and mine eyes had seen it:

My child, I am with you and I love you. I desire to bless each of My children abundantly. My riches you cannot comprehend. They are worth far more than the most money you could ever imagine. My riches are joy unspeakable and they are full of glory. It is complete peace. It is having My wisdom, It is being in My presence constantly, moving as I move, loving as I love. Your life would be full, filled with Me. Focus on Me, the pearl of great price.

I will bless your day and the visits you will make. Speak My words of faith and comfort to those you meet, yes, declare My goodness. The world needs to hear how I bless My people.

NOVEMBER 4

Daily Reading: Genesis 27

Proverbs 13:22   A good man leaveth an inheritance to his children's children: and the wealth of the sinner is laid up for the just.

My children you are My son and My daughter. You have inherited all that I have. Parents leave an inheritance to their children. You are My children and I am your Father. I delight to pour out My blessings upon you. An inheritance is received after a death and this inheritance from Me was made available because of Jesus' death. You entered into My family by birth, by being born again. You enter into My kingdom by death, death to the old nature with all it's worldly and fleshly desires.

I rejoice that you have both entered My kingdom. I will pour out My blessings, which is your inheritance, upon you. I will be with you this day.

NOVEMBER 5

Daily Reading: Acts 25: 1-12

Revelation 12: 10   *And I heard a loud voice saying in heaven, Now is come salvation, and strength, and the kingdom of our God, and the power of His Christ: for the accuser of our brethren is cast down, which accused them before our God day and night.*

I love you both. You are both in the hollow of My hand. Storms may rage and winds may blow, but in My hand you are safe. Remember, I look not on the outward appearance, but I look at the heart. I look at the intent and purposes of the heart. Satan is the accuser of the brethren and where he can bring railings he will.

Now I say to you again, keep your eyes on Me, not on the situation you are going through or your circumstances. Trust Me this day. I have only the best in store for you.

NOVEMBER 6

Daily Reading: Acts 11:1-18

Genesis 11:6   *And the Lord said, Behold, the people is one, and they have all one language: and this they begin to do: and now nothing will be restrained from them, which they have imagined to do.*

Learn to bring every problem, every situation, even every happening in your life to Me. I rejoice when you rejoice and I cry when you cry. I am a part of you and you are a part of Me. So then, how could you leave Me out of anything pertaining to your life?

I am doing a good work in your life. Those that come to Me with a pure heart, I will in no wise cast out. I will bring unity in My body. My kingdom cannot be a divided kingdom for a divided kingdom will fall. Neither am I coming for a fragmented bride, but she will be whole and pure, undefiled from the world. Rejoice because you have a part in this!

I am rebuilding and restoring My body. In every situation that you go through I will be there to help you and to strengthen you, and you will bring praise to My name.

NOVEMBER 7

Daily Reading: Romans 6

Romans 13:14   *But put ye on the Lord Jesus Christ, and make not provision for the flesh, to fulfil the lusts thereof.*

My son, My daughter, I want to reveal more and more of My Word to you. There are many things still hidden in My Word that I desire to show you. Seek Me and spend time with Me. Be selective in your television watching for when you put on the world you will reap the world. When you put Me on, I will grow in you. People will see whatever is growing in you.

I desire to see your thoughts, body, soul and spirit all controlled by Me, yielded to My will and purposes. Flesh cannot satisfy the needs of the spirit, only My Word can do that. I love you and I will be with you this day.

NOVEMBER 8

Daily Reading: Psalm 63

Psalm 63:1   *0 God, Thou art my God; early will I seek Thee: my soul thirsteth for Thee, my flesh longeth for Thee in a dry and thirsty land, where no water is;*

My child I am here and I love you. You have taken your eyes off me and put them on your circumstances. I love you and I will not lead you where I will not also be. Sometimes it may seem like you are not going forward, but you are. I am leading you onward.

It may seem just like the psalmist said, that you are going through a dry and thirsty land but remember the water is there deep under the soil. Your surroundings and circumstances may seem dry and thirsty, but I am your living water, waiting to be tapped into. I cause the desert to bloom and produce fruit. My child whatever the circumstance, I am there with you. Will you seek and spend time with Me today?

NOVEMBER 9

Daily Reading: 1 Thessalonians 4: 1-12

Romans 8:29   *For whom He did foreknow, He also did predestinate to be conformed to the image of His Son, that He might be the first born among many brethren.*

My child, I love you. I am pleased with you. I am at work in your life changing you bit by bit. Continue to spend time with Me and My Word, and I will continue to do My work in your life. Do not get down about failures or mistakes in your life. Confess them to Me and I will change them.

My child many changes are taking place and I am doing a good work in you. More and more you are changing into My image. Rejoice and be happy over what I am doing in your life for every change that makes you more into My likeness brings great rejoicing in heaven. I will be with you this day.

NOVEMBER 10

Daily Reading: James 3

James 3:2   *For in many things we offend all. If any man offend not in word, the same is a perfect man, and able also to bridle the whole body.*

My child, I am with you and I will always love you, but you have need to bridle your tongue. Words can so quickly cut someone down and hurt and destroy them. You have need to rest in Me. I am in control and the remarks you so quickly make are not going to change situations. They often leave wounded people in their wake.

It is in spending time with Me in prayer that you will see things differently. I am the one who opens and closes doors. Man can bring forth an abundance of thoughts but only that which comes from Me, will have My blessing. Be comforted, I have not cast you aside.

Purpose in your heart to speak forth that which I would have you speak. You desire a pure heart and I am working a purity within you. Put on the garment of praise for the spirit of heaviness. Rejoice in Me today!

NOVEMBER 11

Daily Reading: Song of Solomon 4:1-7,5:8-16

Ephesians 5:33   *Nevertheless let every one of you in, particular so love his wife even as himself; and the wife see that she reverence her husband.*

Encourage your partner with all your heart. Be like Me, I love you and I encourage your heart when it needs it. I encouraged My disciples when they needed to hear it. You are in a special place. I have made you both one, a helpmeet to one another. Minister that help to each other.

You have confidence in him (her) and that is good, but he (she) needs to hear it. You know him (her) better than anyone else. You know his (her) insecurities, minister in that area and build him (her) up. You have seen Me do a great work in him (her), but you do not often tell him (her) that he (she) has grown tremendously. Tell him (her) and give him (her) much love. My annointing is upon both of you.

NOVEMBER 12

Daily Reading: James 5:7-20

James 5:16   *Confess your faults one to another, and pray one for another, that ye may be healed. The effectual fervent prayer of a righteous man availeth much.*

My children, I love you. To be able to meet the need of someone else, you must put yourself aside. Bringing yourself into the picture will cause feelings of frustration in the other person. Bringing self into a situation shows that our heart is not really desiring to help meet the other's needs, just our own.

I have given you to each other to make my body complete, to provide what is missing. Together you are whole. That is why dwelling in self cannot be the answer. In Me you can meet each other's needs. When one needs to talk the other needs to listen, instead of defending yourself. When you are not able to help each other, ask Me for the solution for the other person. That is putting aside self. You will both be blessed by it. Pray much for one another. I will be with you today.

NOVEMBER 13

Daily Reading: 1 Kings 12:1-16

Psalm I:Ia   *Blessed is the man that walketh not in the counsel of the ungodly.*

My people, I love you. You are all a part of My body. My desire is that My body would minister to one another. I have placed within My body counselors, filled with My wisdom.

It is important, My people, that you receive godly counsel. The counsel of the world has its roots in humanism. There will be no encouragement to lay down self or to let Me deal in the situation and many times it will contradict My word. I have placed within my counselors a spirit of wisdom to give godly advice to those who are in need.

Continue to look in My Word for more of My truth and wisdom. There is an answer for every need and every problem. I will be with you this day.

NOVEMBER 14

Daily Reading: Revelation 5:1-9, 20:11-15

Psalm 139:16   *Thine eyes did see my substance, yet being unperfeet; and in Thy book all my members were written, which in continuance were fashioned, when as yet there was none of them.*

My child, I love you. Your life is like this book. Daily I am writing on the pages of your heart. I seek continual fellowship with you. You have need of more of Me. No one ever has enough of Me.

Your life is like this book because I continue to start new chapters in your life, and bring new things your way. I need for you to seek Me and My fellowship. How can I speak to you and minister to you if you do not come to Me? I desire close communion with you. I love you My child and it hurts and grieves Me when you draw away from fellowship with Me. Turn your heart to Me this day and let My peace rule in your heart.

NOVEMBER 15

Daily Reading: Romans 4:13-25

2 Cor. 1:20   *For all the promises of God in Hint are yea, and in Him Amen, unto the glory of God by us.*

My child I go ever before you and I love you. My ways are so different from your ways. Your vision is so limited whereas My vision sees the end from the beginning. All that I have spoken will come to pass. Continue to keep your eyes on Me, so you will not feel disappointed.

I am in control and I am moving you on towards the goal I have placed before you. The enemy is out to rob you. You will not have to wait forever. The enemy is telling you those lies. You are afraid to voice My promises anymore because you are beginning to doubt them inyour heart. Give Me your doubts. Rejoice in Me today and the enemy will flee away from you.

NOVEMBER 16

Daily Reading: Proverbs 31:10-31

Titus 2:4,5   *That they may teach the young women to be sober, to love their husbands, to love their children, To be discreet, chaste, keepers at home, good, obedient to their own husbands, that the word of God be not blasphemed.*

My daughter I am in you, beside you, around you, and I love you. I will be with you today. Do the things that are at hand and I will bless you in it. An orderly and neat home is a blessing from Me, it will bring peace and rest to those who enter therein. My joy will reign. in your home.

I desire to bless your basket and your store. My blessings are the provisions and inheritance for My children. You are able to be a blessing in your home, in how you take care of your home and family. Do not take them for granted, but daily praise Me for them.

NOVEMBER 17

Daily Reading: Psalm 143

Psalm 143:10   Teach me to do Thy will; for Thou art my God: Thy Spirit is good; lead me into the land of uprightness.

My child I am with you and I love you. I ani pleased that you desire to do My will. I must increase and you must decrease. Laying down your will for My will is the sacrifice you must make, but I will enable you to do it.

I am doing a good work in your life. There will be a strong foundation. Brick by brick the walls will go up. As you continue to lay down your will and yield to My leading, you will be built up in Me. I will be with you this day and bless you. Do what is at hand to do.

NOVEMBER 18

Daily Reading: 1 Kings 3 :3-15

Matthew 6:33   But seek ye first the kingdom of God, and His righteousness; and all these things shall be added unto you.

My child, I love you. It is good that you seek My direction for your life at this time. You are at a crossroad in your life and you need My wisdom to make a decision. You do not desire leanness in your soul, but your top priority is to be true to the calling I have placed in your life.

You sensed right, the choice is yours. I am pleased that you desire My will in your life. Solomon was placed before a choice and he chose wisdom and I blessed him because of it. When you choose My way there will not be leanness in your soul.

Your desire for more funds so that you can be a blessing unto others is not wrong. Whatever you place on the altar of sacrifice will release My hand of blessing in your life. I will not be in debt to any man. Rest in this and watch Me open doors for you.

NOVEMBER 19

Daily Reading: Hebrews 7:1-10

Luke 15:31　　　*And he said unto him, Son, thou art ever with me, and all that I have is thine*

Genesis 14:20　　*And blessed be the most high God, which hath delivered thine enemies into thine hand. And he gave him tithes of all.*

My son and My daughter, I love you. You have a desire in your heart to bless your children. I have that same desire. You are My children, My son and My daughter. My heart too is busy with ways to bless you. All that is mine is yours. Enter into My promises, My blessings for you. The world and other Christians will be amazed at how rich you will be in Me.

I prospered Abraham abundantly. He was a sojourner in the land and yet I blessed him so much that he was a living testimony to all the inhabitants around him. You are a citizen of the kingdom of heaven and a sojourner here in this world, but I desire to make you a testimony for all those around you. Abraham knew it was his God that made him rich and he paid tithes to Melchizedek the priest. I will make you rich and you will bring tithes to your local church. I will be with you this day.

NOVEMBER 20

Daily Reading: Matthew 6:5-15

Matthew 6:6　　*But thou, when thou prayest, enter into thy closet, and when thou hast shut thy door, pray to thy Father which is in secret; and thy Father which seeth in secret shall reward thee openly.*

My son, I love you. I see the desire in your heart to be able to pray more effectively. First come to Me with your whole heart because you want to, not because it is now time to pray. You believe in Me and desire My whole attention and I desire yours.

When you do not know what to pray for, start praising Me for who I am. I love you and I desire to be told that you love Me without wanting something from Me. Praise will release My hand of blessing more and more.

Prayer is sharing and releasing what is in your heart to Me. The more you share with Me, the more I share with you. My ears are always open to the cries of My people. I will be listening for your voice today. Will you come to Me in prayer?

NOVEMBER 21

Daily Reading: Philippians 3:13-21

Matt. 28:19,20   *Go ye therefore, and teach all nations, baptizing them in the name of the Father, and of the Son, and of the Holy Ghost: Teaching them to observe all things whatsoever I have com man ded you: and Lo, I am with you alway, even unto the end of the world. Amen!*

My child, I love you. Seek to spend more time with Me. It is important that you be well established in My Word and in My principles. In order to teach others effectively, it must be in operation in your own life. My son walked in everything that he taught.

I am with you this day. Draw near to Me. Keep your eyes and thoughts focused on Me. I have won every battle and gained the victory over hell, Satan and all his host. Now you can walk in freedom. My word can reign and rule in your life completely. I will use you to draw others into My kingdom and teach them to know Me and My Word. Rejoice before Me this day.

NOVEMBER 22

Daily Reading: Acts 4:5-12,5:12-16

Acts 9:34   *And Peter said unto him, Aeneas, Jesus Christ maketh thee whole: arise, and make thy bed. And he arose immediately.*

John 14:12   *Verily, verily, I say unto you, He that believeth on Me, the works that I do shall he do also; and greater works than these shall he do; because I go unto My Father.*

My child, I love you. I take pleasure in your praises. You need to stay close to My side. I will be with you this day. In yourself you will have nothing to give, but I in you do have something to give, to impart to those in need. Concentrate on My presence. It's not by might, it's not by power, but it is by My Spirit. I am the answer to the needs of each and every individual.

Leave every problem in My hands. When your mind becomes occupied with problems and needs, then you have not placed them in My care. Worship Me, love Me and spend time with Me for it will renew your mind.

NOVEMBER 23

Daily Reading: Ephesians 4:17-32

Ephesians 4:23   *And be renewed in the spirit of your mind;*

My people I would gladly share My thoughts with you, you are My beloved. I am at work in this area. My light is penetrating the darkness and My light is spreading. People in darkness are drawn to the light.

Purify yourselves and allow no darkness to enter in by watching wrong movies or by thinking impure thoughts. Put aside those things that so easily beset you. Become stronger and bolder in Me. Set your affection on things above, meaning you will your will to love Me, My words, My works and My will. You will your will to hate what I hate. It is a matter of the will. More and more blessings of My kingdom are waiting for you when you purpose to do this. I love you and will be with you this day.

NOVEMBER 24

Daily Reading: Isaiah 35

Isaiah 54:14   In righteousness shalt thou be established: thou shalt be far from oppression; for thou shalt not fear: and front terror; for it shall not come near thee.

My son, My daughter, you cannot enter into My rest completely until you have let go of all your fears. You will eventually experience the thing you fear, because Satan has blinded you. He has had you build on that thought of fear. Every time you give way to that thought of fear, you are incubating Satan's thoughts and building them into existence. To get rid of the fear eventually you will do the very thing that you had feared, to prove something to yourself and you will see what Satan has accomplished. It was his desire all the time.

I love you so much and I desire to set you free from all your fears. Freedom from torments and bondages and oppression is the heritage for My children, for you. Rest in Me today and give Me your fears.

NOVEMBER 25

Daily Reading: Psalm 27

Psalm 27:1   The Lord is my light and my salvation; Whom shall I fear? The Lord is the strength of my life; of whom shall I be afraid?

I see that there is turmoil and unrest in your soul because there is fear in your life. I am at work in your life to set you free from fears, even hidden fears. I am in control of your life and I will perfect all that concerns you.

I am not a hard taskmaster. Satan would weigh you down. He would have you respond to his thoughts of fear, guilt, anger, etc., for then his kingdom will be advanced. Let My peace, love and joy rule in your heart this day. Rejoice in Me.

NOVEMBER 26

Daily Reading: Psalm 139

Psalm 139: 14   I will praise thee; for I am fearfully and wonderfully made: marvellous are Thy works; and that my soul knoweth right well.

My child, I love you. I knew you long before you existed. I made you. As it is written in My Word, I covered you. You have put on this body and someday you will leave it behind again. You came from Me and you will return to Me.

I created you to do a work for Me, to bring glory and praise to My name. I desire communion and fellowship with you. As you rejoice in Me, I rejoice in you. What you give to Me, I will give back to you. First I gave you life, physical life, then I gave you spiritual life. Twice I have given you life. Without Me you were nothing. I desire My fullness to flow through you.

Rejoice and praise Me continually for what I am doing in you, in My body the Church and in this world.

NOVEMBER 27

Daily Reading: 2 Corinthians 9

2 Corinthians 9:8   And God is able to make all grace abound toward you; that ye, always having all sufficiency in all things, may abound to every good work:

The words that I speak will bring release, but many times you spend more time on your own thoughts which bring bondage. Be released in Me. I will set you free from all anxieties and fears. I have placed My arms of protection around you to keep you safe.

Always look to ME. Do not focus your eyes or thoughts upon people or circumstances. I will lead you. The road may be narrow, but it will be filled with My blessing. My storehouse is filled and I will meet your needs according to My riches in glory. It will be according to My riches, not according to your need. Draw from Me, My supply will never run out. Go in My peace and blessing this day.

NOVEMBER 28

Daily Reading: Exodus 18

Exodus 18:19   *Hearken now unto my voice, I will give thee counsel, and God shall be with thee: Be thou for the people to Godward, that thou mayest bring the causes unto God:*

My child, I love you. Commit all things to Me and do not let any unrest minister to your soul. I will give you a spirit of wisdom and counsel this day. Do not worry about people's opinion of you. Rest in Me.

When you are obedient to what I ask of you, I will be pleased and that is all that matters. I will also work in men's hearts to know that I am pleased with you. That which you gaze upon, you will become. When you gaze only on problems you will receive problems, when you gaze on Me you will become like Me and receive answers to the problems. I will be with you this day. Share Me with others.

NOVEMBER 29

Daily Reading: John 8:1-11

Luke 9:56a   *For the Son of man is not come to destroy men's lives, but to save them.*

John 8:11b   *Neither do I condemn thee: go, and sin no more.*

I will send people your way for you to minister to. Do not look at them through natural eyes, but ask Me how I see them and how I would respond to a particular person. I respond in love. The strongest force cannot stand before love. In the world's way of thinking, I do things backwards, such as give and it shall be given unto you. But it is the world that is backwards. My kingdom is not motivated by selfish desires but by love. Love does not think of self, but of the other person. Love those I send your way, for surely they will come, even now they are coming. Give and it shall be given unto you, good measure, pressed down and running over. Minister in My love this day for I will be with you.

NOVEMBER 30

Daily Reading: Mark 10: 13-16, 46-52

2 Cor. 3:18   *But we all, with open face beholding as in a glass the glory of the Lord, are changed into the same image from glory to glory, even as by the Spirit of the Lord.*

My child, I love you perfectly, Look for Me in others and concentrate on that. You do not find it hard to love Me. When you look for Me in others and concentrate on the part that is Me, it will not be difficult to love as I love. When you look at human failings and shortcomings you will find it difficult to love them as I love them. Human failings and short comings make you shortsighted. Your eyes become focused on a person instead of on Me, your God. In Me and with Me your vision has no limit.

Without a vision My people are limited and downcast, and eventually it can destroy them. Let Me continue to give you vision and insight into what I am doing in each person. I am making My people into My perfect body. Each part is perfect and is needed to make up the whole body, to be the express image of My glory!

DECEMBER I

Daily Reading: 2 Peter 1

2 Peter 1:3   *According as His divine power hath given unto us all things that pertain unto life and godliness, through the knowledge of Him that hath called us to glory and virtue:*

My child, I am with you and I will bless you. I am doing a work in you. Continually you are going forward, pressing into My kingdom and into My treasures. Your habitation is with men, but not of men. You are a stranger and sojourner in this world. My kingdom is a spiritual kingdom with love, peace, joy etc. Set Me constantly before your eyes as your example for everything.

Learn of Me. Guard your relationship with Me, never take it for granted, but feed and nurse it. In My kingdom you shall have fullness of joy and riches unspeakable. Riches and joy coming from Me.

DECEMBER 2

Daily Reading: John 20: 19-31

John 20:29   *Jesus saith unto him, Thomas, because thou hast seen Me, thou hast believed: blessed are they that have not seen, and yet have believed.*

My child, I love you. You are observing many things. Observing is fine, but do not let negative questions bring in negative fears. I desire to set you free from all your fears. I desire for you to trust Me completely. Your trust should be so complete that when I speak, you will immediately follow without doubting or wondering how it will all work out. I know the end from the beginning.

Mistakes may have been made, but I do not condemn people for them. I look at the motive and content of the heart. Follow Me, I am doing a good work in you.

DECEMBER 3

Daily Reading: Acts 18

Acts 18:26   *And he began to speak boldly in the synagogue: whom when Aquila and Priscilla had heard, they took him unto them, and expounded unto him the way of God more perfectly.*

My son and My daughter, I love you and I am pleased with you. Both of you are working in My kingdom to help set the captives free. I choose to work through My body, through the vessels I have chosen. I have called you both to set the captives free in My name.

A great and effectual door is opening for you both. Be faithful unto Me, the author and finisher of your faith. When I open a door, no man can shut it and when I close a door, no man can open it. Trust Me and lean not to your own understanding, but acknowledge Me in all your ways and I will direct your paths. I will be with you this day and bless you.

DECEMBER 4

Daily Reading: Ezekiel 34:11-31

Ezekiel 34: 11   *For thus saith the Lord God; Behold, I, even I, will both search My sheep, and seek them out.*

Despise not the day of small beginnings. I have many people in this area, but they are scattered because they know not who their shepherd is and they know not the safety of the confines of the sheepfold. I will bring My sheep together. My hand is on this place for your good.

Praise Me and expect great things, the more you expect Me to do, the more I will do. I am a great God, there is nothing to difficult for Me and I will have a Church that will minister to the total man, in his spirit, soul and body. Ask Me for much for I delight to give to My body. Keep your eyes on Me and you will never be disappointed. I love you and I delight in meeting your expectations this day.

DECEMBER 5

Daily Reading: Romans 13

Hebrews 13:17   *Obey them that have the role over you, and submit yourselves: for they watch for your souls, as they that must give account, thatthey may do it with joy, and not with grief: for that is unprofitable for you.*

My son, My daughter, you must learn to submit to authority. This is not difficult for those who have grown up in a home that is in order. When parents love Me and love their children then those children will not have any problems submitting to their authority.

Now I have placed others in authority over you. Do not try to override this authority because your eyes are on the person and you see his human character and failings. Reason will speak to you and say, "you can do this so much better." My people realize that those are the very times I am trying to work something out in your life. My authority over you is my instrument in your life for good.

Recognize that I am over all the authority in your life. When you submit to those over you, you are really submitting to Me. I love you.

DECEMBER 6

Daily Reading: Malachi 3:16-18,4

Acts 2:44   *And all that believed were together, and had all things common;*

My child, I love you. Be secure in that love. You do not need to question that love. You question whether others in My body love you like I do.

Sometimes you put up a wall when fellowship is mentioned because you like your individuality. You are comfortable with Me, but not always with everyone else in the body. They do not understand you like I understand you. You fear that they might hurt you whereas I would never hurt you. Let Me lead you in this. Your life is hid in Me. There is a need for close fellowship in the body. Love the brethren and they will love you. Seek My fellowship this day.

DECEMBER 7

Daily Reading: Matthew 20:17-28

2 Cor. 10:5   *Casting down imaginations, and every high thing that exalteth itself against the knowledge of God, and bringing into captivity every thought to the obedience of Christ;*

My child, I love you. You sometimes, so quickly, take your eyes off Me and focus them on your circumstances. Outwardly, you are voicing the thoughts that come to your mind, but the whole time you are talking, deep in your heart you know the answer. Listen to your heart more and bring your thoughts into captivity to Me.

Whatever you do should be done as unto Me. If you do it as unto people, your flesh will be ministered to, but if you do it as unto Me, your spirit will be ministered to. To grow closer unto Me, your flesh is being denied so your spirit can grow. Continue to look to Me for I am pleased with you. I will be with you today.

DECEMBER 8

Daily Reading: Romans 10

Romans 10:17   *So then faith cometh by hearing, and hearing by the word of God.*

v.16a   *But they have not all obeyed the gospel.*

My son, My daughter, continue to abide in My word. My word will lead and guide you. Seek Me for My revelation and the illumination of My Holy Spirit in every situation of your life. I will continue to speak to you, but you must continue to be faithful and obedient to My word.

There is much in store for My body, but I need people who will hear My word and respond to it. Continue to seek My guidance in your prayer time with Me and be obedient to what I say to you. This will cause your faith to grow and bear much fruit in your life. Abide in My presence this day and listen for My voice, I love you.

DECEMBER 9
Daily Reading: 2 Corinthians 6:1-13

Psalm 4:1   *Hear me when I call, O God of my righteousness: Thou hast enlarged me when I was in distress; have mercy upon me, and hear my prayer.*

My child I desire to draw close to you and for you to draw close to Me. I desire for you to seek Me constantly and to give Me pre-eminence.

I love you. Continue to encourage and strengthen the brethren. You bring praise and glory to My name when you follow after Me with your whole heart. Singleness of heart, soul and mind is what I am after.

I have also been enlarging your tent pegs. You must lay down the hurt caused by rejection. In My eyes you were never a failure, but a child who was obedient to My call regardless of the cost. Yes, it hurt, but I too suffered hurt and rejection. I am at work in your life moving you on, making you stronger and enabling you to do greater things. Rejoice in Me this day for My love is keeping you and causing you to grow in Me.

DECEMBER 10
Daily Reading: Matthew 5: 1-12

Matthew 5:8   *Blessed are the pure in heart: for they shall see God.*

My son, My daughter, I love you. I desire for you to have a pure heart. A heart totally pleasing to Me where all of self has been put aside. I can freely flow through such a heart. It is a heart that loves Me above all else. It is a heart totally committed to Me to move only when I say so. I desire for you to have such a heart.

Let Me work these desires in your heart. Give Me the right to do this in your heart and I will do the rest. My love, peace and joy will be your portion.

DECEMBER 11

Daily Reading: Acts 20: 17-38

Acts 20:19   *Serving the Lord with all humility of mind, and with many tears, and temptations, which befell me by the lying in wait of the Jews.*

My son, My daughter, pray for a release of emotions so that My love can flow unhindered through you, doing what it was meant to do. Let My love loose. There is no other area Satan is working as hard on as to keep love bound and hidden. He hates love, he can only hate.

Love is expressed through your actions and through your emotions. Your actions alone are not sufficient and your emotions alone are not sufficient, but a perfect balance and harmony together is necessary. Jesus wept at Lazarus' tomb and the people said, "See how he loved him".

Desire to have that kind of love for My body. To have that, you must totally yield your emotions to Me, for me to bring every bondage and restraint down, to become totally open so that my tears can flow down your face, to be used for My glory and honour and praise. I will be with you this day.

DECEMBER 12

Daily Reading: John 8:20-38

John 8:32   *And ye shall know the truth, and the truth shall make you free.*

My child, I am at work in your life to set you free. Do not fear My dealings. You see me as a judge waiting to hand out punishment to you. Actually it is the opposite, I love you so much that I desire to set you free, so you can hear My voice and enter into all the blessings that I have for you. My dealings are not a form of punishment, but rather a form of upbuilding.

With all these fears in your life you will never fully understand My love. Perfect love casts out fear. Fear brings bondage and unrest to your soul. I desire for you to experience freedom, peace and rest.

DECEMBER 13

Daily Reading: Judges 7:1-8

Zephaniah 3: 13   The remnant of Israel shall not do iniquity, nor speak lies; neither shall a deceitful tongue be found in their mouth: for they shall feed and lie down, and none shall make them afraid.

My people I love you. I desire to set all My people free from bondages and snares of the enemy. I desire to set you completely free. True purity can come to the heart when all evil is removed. I am cleansing My body. The kingdom of darkness has to leave My people. It is slowly being defeated.

Fear is the opposite of faith. My people must be set free from fear so they can move in My faith. I had to deal with those fears in your life because they were robbing you and they could have eventually destroyed you.

I love you so much and I have given you those to stand along side of you, to encourage you, to help and minister to you. I will be with you today.

DECEMBER 14

Daily Reading: Romans 8:1-8, Ephesians 6:5-9

Ephesians 6:6,7   Not with eyeservice, as menpleasers; but as servants of Christ, doing the will of God from the heart; With good will doing service, as to the Lord, and not to men:

My son, I love you. You desire man's acceptance and man's recognition but that does not really matter. What matters is that you do things to please Me. I am the one who rewards you and sets you in place. I look upon the heart, therefore if things are done for the wrong motive and yes, they can be, My blessing will not be upon it. I see what you do in secret as well as what you do openly and I the Lord reward openly.

Strive to keep your heart pure, not to be a man pleaser, but do all things as unto Me. Do not seek man's approval for only My approval will be a blessing in your life. My approval is with you and it is not conditional like man's. Rejoice in My goodness for My kindness is everlasting. I will be with you today.

DECEMBER 15

Daily Reading: Hebrews 6

Eph. 4:14a,15   *That we henceforth be no more children, tossed to and fro,*
But speaking the truth in love, may grow up into Him in all
things, which is the head, even Christ:

My son, My daughter, you are precious to me. Just as your children become more and more precious to you, so do you to Me. Love grows and relationships must grow. Your walk with Me must grow richer and deeper.

Your trust in Me is growing continually. At one time you had no patience to wait for something to happen, but now you know that what I say I will do. It will happen in My timing and it shall be accomplished. My love is always reaching out to you.

It is the negative thoughts that you give way to, that separate you from Me. When you give way to those feelings and thoughts, I step into the background because I do not minister them and they are given pre-eminence. Renew yourself in Me today.

DECEMBER 16

Daily Reading: Romans 14

Romans 14:17   *For the kingdom of God is not meat and drink; but*
righteousness, and peace, and joy in the Holy Ghost.

I love you. I am your Lord and your King. You belong to My kingdom. My kingdom is not from this world. You live in the world, but you are not a part of this worldly kingdom.

My kingdom principles are the opposite from the world's principles. The world says hate when I say love. The world says take when I say give. Dying to self is necessary for you to be a part of My kingdom because the old self was part of the world's system. My kingdom does not consist of flesh and blood, but peace and righteousness and joy.

DECEMBER 17

Daily Reading: Zephaniah 3:8-20

Mark 16:17   *And these signs shall follow them that believe; In my name shall they cast out devils; they shall speak with new tongues;*

My child, this day I will be with you, I love you and I am rejoicing with you. I rejoice when you are obedient to my word and when you use the keys I have given you to set the captives free. Share with others that which I share with you. My word will not return void. A people that will know my word and hear my word will be raised up.

A remnant will rise up and they will praise and obey me. This remnant will grow and prosper even in the midst of difficult times because I will constantly lead and guide them. My words will be a lamp before their feet and a light shining on the way before them.

DECEMBER 18

Daily Reading: Luke 7:36-50

1 John 3:18   *My little children, let us not love in word, neither in tongue; but in deed and in truth.*

I am your King and that makes you a part of My kingdom. You do not belong to an earthly kingdom, but to a heavenly kingdom. More and more you must think like Me, be like Me, act like Me and do like Me.

My kingdom is a kingdom of love. I love you and you love Me. I do not force My subjects, but because they are motivated by love, they respond out of love. Satan uses force and manipulates a person's will, but I leave you a free will and I will continue to woo you with My love. My love must become the motive which moves you at all times. Love gives all. Will you respond to My love today?

DECEMBER 19

Daily Reading: Isaiah 61

Isaiah 61:11   *For as the earth bringeth forth her bud, and as the garden causeth the things that are sown in it to spring forth; so the Lord God will cause righteousness and praise to spring forth before all the nations.*

My sons and My daughters, I am with you and I love each one of you. I have been laying a foundation in your lives. This foundation will be built upon in this coming year. I will do a work in each member of My body.

Many have hurts that have been buried and covered over to be forgotten, but this cannot be because the wound is still there and it will affect your relationship with one another. I will uncover the hurts and pour in the oil and the wine, then it can be completely healed never to bother you again.

There are some who are in bondage because of the past. I have forgiven you your sins of the past, but when they took place, you opened the door to the tormentors and they have not been cast out. Some of you have iniquities in your life because of the sins of your forefathers. I desire to see you set free from these curses. They have been weights around your neck hindering you on the course I have set before you.

Yes, you will see My hand at work in your lives and in My body, the Church. Rejoice, I am coming for a glorious Church, holy and without blemish, spot or wrinkle. Again, I say, Rejoice!!!

DECEMBER 20

Daily Reading: Hebrews 10:22-39

Philippians 1:6   *Being confident of this very thing, that He which hath begun a good work in you will perform it until the day of Jesus Christ:*

My son and My daughter, you are My children. I love you. You have grown in My ways. I have seen you grow and mature and I am pleased. Do not stop here, all of life will be a training and a growing and a perfecting until the time you come home to Me.

Sometimes you desire to draw back but you must never do that. Continue to press in. I will not ask you to walk where I have not gone before you. Keep your eyes on Me at all times for I order your days. I will bless you today.

DECEMBER 21

Daily Reading: Exodus 4:1-20

Exodus 4:11.12   *And the Lord said unto him, Who hath made man's mouth? Or who maketh the dumb, or deaf, or the seeing, or the blind? Have not I the Lord? Now therefore go, and I will be with thy mouth, and teach thee what thou shalt say.*

Rest in Me this day. I will be with you this whole day. Do not strive in your mind, but rest in Me. I am asking you to share the word, that I gave you, with My people.

Do not fear men. My peace shall rule in your heart and you will be amazed. Fear of men will bring a snare to your soul. Fear is not of Me. You are My mouthpiece that I choose to use. Rise in obedience to My word. Obeying My word in your life brings My blessing and My joy. I love you.

DECEMBER 22

Daily Reading: Luke 2:25-39

John 14:27   *Peace I leave with you, My peace I give unto you: not as the world giveth, give I unto you. Let not your heart be troubled, neither let it be afraid.*

My child, I love you. Relax in Me, you are caught up in the busyness of the season. All things will be accomplished and finished. Seek Me this season. It is because of My Son Jesus that you are celebrating Christmas. He came to bring peace to your soul.

It is good that you let people know you care at this time of the year. Let My love shine before you. I am uniting hearts and giving you all a greater love and understanding for one another. I am the reason you are celebrating. Rejoice in Me and with one another.

DECEMBER 23

Daily Reading: Proverbs 24:30-34, 26: 13-16

Romans 14:6a   *He that regardeth the day, regardeth it unto the Lord; and he that regardeth not the day, to the Lord he doth not regard it.*

My child, I love you. I will be with you today. This day belongs to Me, but I give it to you freely. All time is Mine, but I give it to you to use and to enjoy. Use your time wisely for that which is wasted can never be recovered. I am pleased that you sought to spend this time with Me.

Spring will come again and the winter season will be over before you realize it. I desire for you to bring forth much fruit in the next year. Fruit that is pleasing to the eye and sweet to the taste. Work while it is day, and enjoy your work. It is a gift from Me.

DECEMBER 24

Daily Reading: 1 Corinthians 12: 1-11, 28-31

James 1:17   *Every good gift and every pefect gift is from above, and cometh down from the Father of lights, with whom is no variableness, neither shadow of turning:*

You rejoice because your family is together at this time. That is how I rejoice when My children turn to Me and seek My presence and abide in Me. Have a good day with your family.

It is good to give gifts to one another because you love each other. I love to give gifts to My children. These days strengthen natural ties with your family. When I give gifts to you, it strengthens your ties to Me. You put much thought and care and love into getting these gifts. I care and love in a much greater measure. Try to understand how much I care and how much I love you. Enjoy My presence with one another today.

DECEMBER 25

Daily Reading: Isaiah 9:1-7, Luke 2:6-14

Isaiah 9:6   *For unto us a child is born, unto us a Son is given: and the government shall be upon His shoulder: and His name shall be called Wonderful, Counsellor, The Mighty God, The everlasting Father, The Prince of Peace.*

My child, I love you. I am reining in your heart. I rejoice over you with exceedingly great joy. Today you celebrate My birthday and I rejoice in that, but I rejoice even more because you want to follow Me and love Me with your whole heart.

You have My light within you and that is shining out to a dark and dreary and hurting world. It was prophesied years ago that My light would come and chase the darkness away; that is still happening, you are part of that light. I am that Light.

I will give you a good day with loved ones. Rejoice together in all the blessings you have received from Me. I am the one who has made it all possible!

DECEMBER 26

Daily Reading: Ephesians 5:13-21

Ephesians 5: 18   And be not drunk with wine, wherein is excess; but be filled with the Spirit.

My children, I love you and I am pleased with you. Much of the world is in a stupor today because they are hung over from the world's way of celebrating. My heart aches for them. They know no peace, no joy, no hope and no love, they have only misery today.

You can worship Me and read My Word and be filled with My presence. I rejoice when you bring all your requests before Me. I take delight in doing things for My children. I will give you all a good day together and I will be in the midst of you.

DECEMBER 27

Daily Reading: Numbers 33:1-5,49-56

Psalm 105:43,44   And He brought forth His people with joy, and His chosen with gladness. And gave them the lands of the heathen: and they inherited the labour of the people;

My child I have your life in the palm of My hand. I have led you and guided you to where you are now and the future is in My hand. Trust Me completely for nothing can happen in your lives that has not been ordained by Me. My word is in you and it will lead and guide you.

I am wherever you are. Do not let the cares of the world and everyday things take pre-eminence over Me. I will be with you this day, remain close to Me. What you continually look upon is what you will become, become like Me. I will bless this day.

DECEMBER 28

Daily Reading: Romans 9:18-33

Jeremiah 18:4	*And the vessel that he made of clay was marred in the hand of the potter: so he made it again another vessel, as seemed good to the potter to make it.*
Isaiah 64:8	*But now, O Lord, Thou art our Father; we are the clay, and Thou our potter; and we are all the work of Thy hand.*

My child, I love you very much. I have ordained for each person to have weaknesses in their life so that you will need one another. At one time you could not see this.

You compared yourself to others that had problems you didn't have, so I had to take you to My Word and show you that comparing yourself to others was foolish and it built a false image of self within you. I then had to bring circumstances and much rejection in your life that showed how much you need Me. You began to see yourself as someone who had nothing and without Me is nothing. I used this process to put self to death. You were then willing to hand yourself back to Me to shape you into My identity.

Slowly new life is beginning to be seen and it draws people to you. I have made each one unique and perfect for the plan I have for their life. Your weaknesses will keep you humble and in need of your God. You are what you are in Me because of My grace!

DECEMBER 29

Daily Reading: Numbers 16:1-33

Romans 13:1   *Let every soul be subject unto the higher powers. For there is no power but of God: the powers that be are ordained of God.*

My child, I am here and I love you. I am pleased that you took the time today to spend with Me. I am here each day for you. You need My strength and My covering for each day. It is My covering each day that wards off the enemy. Every dart of the enemy can be repelled by Me.

Look to Me for the coming year. I am in control. The enemy will make it look like he is in control, but never fear, because he is deceptive for I am the victorious one and I have complete control. Do not fall prey to any fear tactics. When thoughts come that minister fear know this; that is never from Me. I will be with you this day.

DECEMBER 30

Daily Reading: Exodus 6:1-13

Esther 4:14   *For if thou altogether holdest thy peace at this time, then*
shall there enlargement and deliverance arise to the Jews
from another place; but thou and thy father's house shall
be destroyed: and who knoweth whether thou art come to
the kingdom for such a time as this?

My child, I love you. You are beginning to sense My timing. Everything I say or do is in regards to eternity. I know the end from the beginning. Do not look at immediate circumstances, but see My hand in the whole situation.

I had spoken to Abraham that his descendants would be in Egypt 400 years. The enemy knew this and he tried to prevent My people from ever coming back to inherit the promised land. He tried to destroy Moses at birth, but I had a long range plan for his life. I knew that the best training for Moses would be to live in Pharaoh's palace. This way he would grow up thinking as a leader rather than a slave.

Your life has been varied, I have taken you where I wanted you, but it was because I have a plan for your life and the best training can be had where I place you. I am still unfolding My plan for your life. Seek Me and acknowledge Me in all your ways and I will direct your paths.

DECEMBER 31

Daily Reading: Revelation 22

Revelation 19:7   *Let us be glad and rejoice, and give honour to Him: for the maniage of the Lamb is come, and His wife hath made herself ready.*

My children, I love you. This may be the last day of the year, but in My plan for your life it is just another day. My promises are faithful and true. My word can be depended on. I have done much in this past year and My work will continue in your life.

Thank Me for everything you have received from My hands, it has all been a token of My love for you. I love My children with an everlasting love.

You Can Hear God's Voice!

By Mark and Patti Virkler, co-authors of "4 Keys to Hearing God's Voice"

Christianity is unique among religions, for it alone offers a personal relationship with the Creator beginning here and now, and lasting throughout eternity. Jesus declared, "This is eternal life – that they may **know God**" (Jn. 17:2). Unfortunately, many in the Church miss the great blessing of fellowship with our Lord because we have lost the ability to recognize His voice within us. Though we have the promise that "My sheep hear My voice," too many believers are starved for that intimate relationship that alone can satisfy the desire of their hearts.

I was one of those sheep who was deaf to his Shepherd until the Lord revealed four very simple keys (found in Habakkuk 2:1, 2) that unlocked the treasure of His voice.

Key #1 – God's voice in your heart often sounds like a flow of spontaneous thoughts.

Habakkuk knew the sound of God speaking to him (Hab. 2:2). Elijah described it as a still, small voice (I Kings 19:12). I had always listened for an inner **audible** voice, and God does speak that way at times. However, I have found that usually, **God's voice comes as spontaneous thoughts, visions, feelings, or impressions.**

For example, haven't you been driving down the road and had **a thought come to you** to pray for a certain person? Didn't you believe it was God telling you to pray? What did God's voice sound like? Was it an audible voice, or was it a spontaneous thought that lit upon your mind?

Experience indicates that we perceive spirit-level communication as spontaneous thoughts, impressions and visions, and Scripture confirms this in many ways. For example, one definition of *paga*, a Hebrew word for intercession, is "a chance encounter or an accidental intersecting." When God lays people on our hearts, He does it through *paga*, a chance-encounter thought "accidentally" intersecting our minds.

Therefore, when you want to hear from God, tune to chance-encounter or spontaneous thoughts.

Key #2 – Become still so you can sense God's flow of thoughts and emotions within.

Habakkuk said, "I will stand on my guard post..." (Hab. 2:1). Habakkuk knew that to hear God's quiet, inner, spontaneous thoughts, he had to first go to a quiet place and still his own thoughts and emotions. Psalm 46:10 encourages us to be still, and know that He is God. There is a deep inner knowing (spontaneous flow) in our spirits that each of us can experience when we quiet our flesh and our minds. If we are not still, we will sense only our own thoughts.

Loving God through a quiet worship song is one very effective way to become still. (Note II Kings 3:15.) After I worship and become silent within, I open myself for that spontaneous flow. If thoughts come of things I have forgotten to do, I write them down and dismiss them. If thoughts of guilt or unworthiness come, I repent thoroughly, receive the washing of the blood of the Lamb, putting on His robe of righteousness, seeing myself spotless before God (Is. 61:10; Col. 1:22).

To receive the pure word of God, it is very important that my heart be properly focused as I become still because my focus is the source of the intuitive flow. If I fix my eyes upon Jesus, the intuitive flow comes from Jesus. But if I fix my gaze upon some desire of my heart, the intuitive flow comes out of that desire. To have a pure flow I must become still and carefully fix my eyes upon Jesus. Again, quietly worshiping the King, and receiving out of the stillness that follows quite easily accomplishes this.

Fix your gaze upon Jesus (Heb. 12:2), becoming quiet in His presence and sharing with Him what is on your heart. Spontaneous thoughts will begin to flow from the throne of God to you, and you will actually be conversing with the King of Kings!

Key #3 – As you pray, fix the eyes of your heart upon Jesus, seeing in the Spirit the dreams and visions of Almighty God.

Habakkuk said, "I will keep watch to see," and God said, "Record the vision" (Hab. 2:1,2). Habakkuk was actually looking for vision as he prayed. He opened the eyes of his heart, and looked into the spirit world to see what God wanted to show him. This is an intriguing idea.

God has always spoken through dreams and visions, and He specifically said that they would come to those upon whom the Holy Spirit is poured out (Acts 2:1-4, 17).

I had never thought of opening the eyes of my heart and looking for vision. However, I have come to believe that this is exactly what God wants me to do. He gave me eyes in my heart to see in the spirit the vision and movement of Almighty God. There is an active spirit world all around us, full of angels, demons, the Holy Spirit, the omnipresent Father, and His omnipresent Son, Jesus. The only reasons for me not to see this reality are unbelief or lack of knowledge.

In order to see, we must look. Daniel saw a vision in his mind and said, "I was looking...I kept looking...I kept looking" (Dan. 7:2,9,13). As I pray, I look for Jesus, and I watch as He speaks to me, doing and saying the things that are on His heart. Many Christians will find that if they will only look, they will see, in the same way they receive spontaneous thoughts. Jesus is Emmanuel, God with us (Matt. 1:23). It is as simple as that. You can see Christ present with you because **Christ *is present with you.*** In fact, the vision may come so easily that you will be tempted to reject it, thinking that it is just you. But if you persist in recording these visions, your doubt will soon be overcome by faith as you recognize that the content of them could only be birthed in Almighty God.

Jesus demonstrated the ability of living out of constant contact with God, declaring that He did nothing on His own initiative, but only what He *saw the Father doing, and heard the Father saying* (Jn. 5:19,20,30). *What an incredible way to live!*

Is it possible for you to live out of divine initiative as Jesus did? Yes! Fix your eyes upon Jesus. The veil has been torn, giving access into the immediate presence of God, and He calls you to draw near (Lk. 23:45; Heb. l0: 19-22). "I pray that the eyes of your heart will be enlightened...."

Key #4 – Journaling, the writing out of your prayers and God's answers, brings great freedom in hearing God's voice.

God told Habakkuk to record the vision (Hab. 2:2). This was not an isolated command. The Scriptures record many examples of individual's prayers and God's replies (e.g. the Psalms, many of the prophets, Revelation).

I call the process "two-way journaling," and I have found it to be a fabulous catalyst for clearly discerning God's inner, spontaneous flow, because as I journal **I am able to write in faith for long periods of time,** simply believing it is God. I know that what I believe I have received from God must be tested. However, testing involves doubt and doubt blocks divine communication, so I do not want to test while I am trying to receive. With journaling, I can receive in faith, knowing that when the flow has ended **I can test and examine it carefully,** making sure that it lines up with Scripture.

You will be amazed when you journal. Doubt may hinder you at first, but throw it off, reminding yourself that it is a biblical concept, and that God is present, speaking to His children. Relax. When we cease **our labors** and enter His rest, God is free to flow (Heb. 4:10). Sit back comfortably, take out your pen and paper, smile, and turn your attention toward the Lord in praise and worship, seeking His face. After you write your question to Him, become still, fixing your gaze on Jesus. You will suddenly have a very good thought. Don't doubt it; simply write it down. Later, as you read your journaling, you, too, will be blessed to discover that you are indeed dialoguing with God.

Some final notes: Knowing God through the Bible is a vital foundation to hearing His voice in your heart, so you must have a solid commitment to knowing and obeying the Scriptures. It is also very important for your growth and safety that you be related to solid, spiritual counselors. All major directional moves that come through journaling should be confirmed by your counselors before you act upon them.

For a complete teaching on this topic, order the book *4 Keys to Hearing God's Voice* at www.CWGministries.org or call 716-681-4896. Online catalog of 60 books by Mark & Patti Virkler as well as 100 college courses through external degree: www.cluonline.com

How to fully internalize this teaching and **make it yours**

PSsssT...
do *you* have a
Personal **S**piritual **T**rainer?

Reach Your Spiritual Goals With a "Personal Spiritual Trainer"

For $1 a day, you can have your own spiritual "coach"!
Everyone needs mentoring—someone who will take time to check in, be a sounding board, make suggestions and keep you motivated to attain your goals. But modern daily life is busy and it's hard to find someone who can make that kind of commitment to you. This is why Life Coaching has become such a large trend—professional advisors who make a career of personal, focused attention and guidance. They're very effective, but not everyone can afford them.

Now you can have your own Personal Spiritual Trainer
Communion With God Ministries is making it possible for anyone who can afford a dollar a day to get the one-on-one input needed to master an area of spiritual growth, be it Bible knowledge, walking in the Spirit, leadership skills, finances, prophecy, parenting, vision and life purpose...whatever area you're ready to work on and master, you can have a Personal Spiritual Trainer to see you through to your goal.

Stay on track with a trainer

If you wanted to get into good physical shape, a personal fitness trainer at a health club could give you the experienced knowledge, objective feedback and encouragement you need to reach your fitness goals. A Personal Spiritual Trainer under the auspices of Communion With God Ministries will give you weekly input and personal attention to keep you on-track and moving forward as you attain your spiritual goals. Specialized training modules  will give you the tools you need to grow in the area you desire.

Master an area of growth in just 3 months

We have created a full slate of specialized training modules (over 100 of them!) that will give you the materials and personal input you need to master an area of spiritual growth—not just "know something about it", but *master* it. In just 90 days.

Just think, a year from now you could have four areas of personal breakthrough established and operating in your life. In fact, there's even opportunity to become a Personal Spiritual Trainer yourself! But let's talk about you first…

Personalized goals, personalized attention

You know what you need most, what inspires you most, what lines up with your overall goals. When you choose from over 100 Spirit-anointed training modules, you'll also be assigned a Personal Spiritual Trainer who will connect with you every week to assist you in grasping and applying the truths and experiences you are absorbing as you work through the material. If you can carve out just 50 minutes a day and a weekly appointment with your Personal Spiritual Trainer—via phone or email, your choice—you'll see breakthrough in that area of your life.

Imagine, you'll reach a milestone in your spiritual growth every three months!

Affordable training, manageable commitment, high-quality coaching
We are committed to the equipping and growth of Christians around the world, moving in the flow of the Holy Spirit's counsel and life-changing power. So we are making key materials available to believers for an enrollment that works out to:

- ◈ **Approximately $1 a day, for materials** (books, trainee notebook, CDs or DVDs, depending on the module),

- ◈ *plus* **the weekly one-on-one encouragement and input of a Personal Spiritual Trainer for another $1 a day.**

For only $99 for 90 days, you get weekly appointments with your Personal Spiritual Trainer.

Your total investment is about $189 for 90 days, which includes powerful, Spirit-anointed training materials.

In only 90 days, you can master an area of personal growth.
(There's even a 30-day money-back guarantee!)

You can enroll today, and step into mastery in your spiritual walk, with a Personal Spiritual Trainer alongside to ensure your success.

Call toll-free: **1-800-466-6961** (716-681-4896 outside the U.S.) for a free consultation to discuss your goals and the modules best suited to help you accomplish them.

We'll have your training materials and the contact information for your Personal Spiritual Trainer in the mail to you within two business days.

More details of how your 3-month training works
For a complete list of training modules, or to read our section of Frequently Asked Questions, go to www.cwgministries. org/pst. You're sure to find helpful, practical material that will propel your spiritual growth in just 3 months. You'll have a spiritual breakthrough in your daily walk *for less than a lot of people spend each day on a cup of coffee!*

Let's Get Started!

The core module for all of our trainees is **Communion With God**. Everyone begins their training here, as it teaches you to clearly hear God's voice, to see vision and to do two-way journaling. These skills will revolutionize your devotional life and are used in every subsequent training module.

You can purchase the module on our website, or call us for assistance at 1-800-466-4941 (U.S. only) or 716-681-4896.

Sign up for this module today!
Simply complete the form online at
www.cwgministries.org/pst

How Far Could You Go

with a Bible School in Your Pocket?

Personal Growth

- From anywhere you are
- No group to join
- Direct to you

Easy to Use

- Video & Audio
- Workbook & book
- Interactive online quizzes

Flexible

- Your time
- Your location
- Your pace

Invite Friends

- Easy to use in group setting
- Complete Training Modules

Transformational

- Marriages improve
- Families change
- Powerful testimonies

Take Your Place in God's Advancing Kingdom!

After you invest two years in our School of the Spirit, completing these 18 Spirit Life modules, we guarantee your life will never be the same!

Christian Leadership
U N I V E R S I T Y™
Bringing the voice of God to your learning experience

School of the Spirit

Can I Really Experience a "School of the Spirit" in My Home? Yes, you can!

- You don't have to go away to a Bible school or a School of Ministry.

- You can live in any city, in any country, attend any church, and still earn a Diploma in Applied Spirituality from Christian Leadership University's School of the Spirit! CLU provides **interactive** Spirit Life Training Modules which feature fully downloadable video training experiences and online quizzes, direct to your laptop, tablet or smart phone.

- You can have your School of the Spirit with you wherever you are!
  You can work through these revelation-based learning modules with your church or small group, with your family or on your own – whatever works best for you!

I've never loved studying and taking courses as much as I am loving my coursework through CLU. God is so amazing!
Linda Geyer
Phoenix, AZ

"Christian Leadership University offers without a doubt the most challenging and rewarding teachings I have ever received. I recommend this school to anyone who is serious about their Christian walk. You will never be the same after you take this journey."
– Rev. Al Morris II

How Is the School of the Spirit Unique?

All 160+ teaching segments are presented from a practical, biblical and spiritual perspective. These are provided through Christian Leadership University – *School of the Spirit*. Each of these scripturally sound, revelation-based modules will enrich your life and the lives of all you share them with. These Spirit Life Training Modules were **birthed and proven in real life struggles and victories**. As you meditate through these modules, the Holy Spirit will give you personal revelation and transformation.

Who Are My Teachers?

Dr. Mark Virkler is President of Christian Leadership University and passionate to train on the laws of the Spirit.

Dr. Andrew Hardy, a British Scholar with a passion that you hear from God as you meditate on the Bible.

Learn more and try our free course sampler today:
www.CLUSchooloftheSpirit.com

Topics and Modules

Knowing God Through the Word

- The Art of Biblical Meditation
- Pentateuch
- History 1 - United Kingdom
- History 2 - Divided Kingdom
- Poetry Books
- Major Prophets
- Life of Christ
- Acts and Epistles
- Epistles and Revelation

"Were not our hearts burning within us...
while He was explaining the Scriptures to us?" (Lk. 24:32)

Living in the Spirit

- Your Extraordinary Life
- Hearing God's Voice
- Counseled by God
- Prayers that Heal the Heart
- Hear God Through Your Dreams
- Living Naturally Supernatural
- How to Walk by the Spirit
- Parenting by Grace

"If we live in the Spirit, let us also walk in the Spirit." (Gal. 5:25)

Empowered by the Spirit

- How to Have Mountain Moving Faith
- Divine Healing Toolbox
- How to Receive the Baptism in the Holy Spirit
- How to Build a Winning Team
- Unleashing Healing Power Through Spirit-Born Emotions

"You will receive power when the Holy Spirit
has come upon you." (Acts 1:8)

Dynamic Physical Health

- Take Charge of Your Health

"I pray you prosper and be in good health,
just as your soul prospers." (3 Jn. 2)

Discover Spirit-Anointed Training Modules

DVDs – CDs – Books – Workbooks:
Available individually or as discounted bundles

Ideal for personal and small group use! The DVDs bring an anointed teacher to your group, while the books and workbooks ensure you internalize the new skills being learned and are completely transformed by them. The CDs allow you to review while driving, working or exercising, and you can even hire a Personal Spiritual Trainer to coach you through the entire training process for $1 a day. Or take it one step further and become a distance learning college student with our instructors!

Available at: www.CWGMinistries.org
Phone: 1-800-466-6961 or 716-681-4896

4 Keys to Hearing God's Voice – 10 sessions

Wouldn't it be wonderful to clearly hear God's voice every single day for the rest of your life? Did you know that God is always speaking to you? Do you know what His voice sounds like? You can receive daily counsel from the Wonderful Counselor Who teaches you how to live in faith, hope and love and Who guides you in cultivating great relationships with family and friends. Discover divine patterns for approaching God and four vital keys that will allow you to clearly hear His voice every day. Intimacy with God will be enhanced as you learn how to discern His voice from other voices which clamor for your attention and to record what God reveals to you using two-way journaling as you confirm it through a variety of methods. You WILL experience Jesus' promise that, "My sheep hear My voice" (Jn. 10:27). Your life will be transformed!

Naturally Supernatural – Releasing Christ Continuously, Easily, Powerfully

How do we naturally let Jesus live through us? How do we "abide in Christ" (or "let go and let God")? How do we move from "self-consciousness" to "Christ-consciousness"? In this series you will discover how to return to God's original design for mankind as was demonstrated by Adam and Eve in the Garden of Eden. Four key truths are discussed in the three sessions, and two journaling times are included in the training experience.

3 sessions – Average length: 35 Minutes

How to Speak in Tongues – It's Easier than Most People Make It!

Mark Virkler shares what God taught him that released the gift of speaking in tongues in his life and leads you into receiving this gift as well.

1 session – Length: 26 Minutes

Hear God Through Your Dreams

– 5 sessions plus follow-up practice sessions

Wouldn't it be nice if you could receive counsel from God every night of your life, even while you sleep? You can, because the Bible declares that God counsels us at night through our dreams (Ps. 16:7)! We will examine the dreams in the Bible to see how they illustrate this principle, and how God speaks to His children through their night visions (Num. 12:6; Acts 2:17). We will explore our own dreams, learning the symbolic language of our hearts in order to discern the divine wisdom they are revealing to us. Let the Holy Spirit be your Teacher as you learn to interpret His messages to you through your dreams!

How to Walk by the Spirit – Defining Spirit Sensations So We Can Walk in the Spirit

It is only as we minister in the anointing of the Holy Spirit that we can effectively touch the hearts of others. This practical course trains you how to sense the Holy Spirit Who lives within you, how to get to know Him as a Person, and how to release His power to heal a hurting people.

9 sessions – Average length: 50 Minutes

Spirit-Anointed Teaching – 3 sessions

Discover how you can be a Spirit-led communicator. As a parent, a co-worker or a friend, you want the skill of sensing another's heart and communicating directly, heart to heart. This training is for everyone! When you teach, you are to make classtime a time of experiencing God and sensing the transmission of the life flow of the precious Holy Spirit among the participants. Learning is to be much more than a study about God. It is to be an experience *with* God. This training will teach you how to make every learning experience or class a time of encounter with the Lord, where each one receives an impartation of the anointing of the Holy Spirit.

Five Fold Team Ministry: Unique Gifts Make Winning Teams!

You will become much more successful by learning to surround yourself with fivefold teams. The Bible declares that in the multitude of counselors there is safety (Prov. 11:14). Discover a practical way to create teams who advise you in every area of your life and to ensure that these people together manifest the five heart motivations of Ephesians 4:11 (apostle, prophet, evangelist, pastor and teacher). When you draw out the input from everyone on your team, you receive a variety of perspectives and a much better overall revelation of how to move forward effectively in whatever area you are pursuing.

Counseled by God – Emotional Wholeness Through Hearing God's Voice

You do not have to hurt forever. There is an end to the pain. A genuine word from the Lord heals the broken-hearted. All the "how to" books can never do what a *rhema* word from God can do for the inner man. We will let God speak to our hearts and counsel us about the basic emotional pressures of life. These include anger, doubt, depression, condemnation and inferiority. We will learn to let God replace these with His opposites, as His voice releases His grace within our hearts. Those whom the Son sets free are free indeed.

13 sessions – Average length: 30 Minutes

Through the Bible – 83 sessions

Wouldn't you love to have an anointed storyteller at your side, opening for you God's unfolding plan for mankind as you journey through the Bible from cover to cover? That is exactly what we have prepared for you as you listen to Dr. Andrew Hardy, a British scholar, masterfully unfold God's Story of Redemption from Genesis to Revelation. As the disciples on the Emmaus road walked with Jesus they said to one another, *"Were not our hearts burning within us while He was speaking to us on the road, while He was explaining the Scriptures to us?"* Likewise, the Holy Spirit can explain the Scriptures to us today, and grant us insight and revelation (Eph. 1:17, 18) as we meditate through Scripture!

Prayers That Heal the Heart – 13 sessions

Are you tired of ineffective prayers for healing? Learn how you can experience complete healing of the wounds in your heart by applying specific prayers to each heart wound. These seven supernatural prayers will allow you to use the language of the heart to break generational sins and curses, sever ungodly soul ties, replace negative beliefs with God's promises, renounce inner vows, receive divine visions, break word curses spoken over you, and cast out every demonic stronghold that has connected itself to these inner wounds. We will teach you how to stay healed by guiding you in an intensive Bible meditation experience where you receive revelation knowledge from God, which closes the door so the adversary cannot return.

Divine Healing Toolbox – Make Healing Prayer More Effective

Discover a host of practical suggestions for how to make prayer for physical healing more effectual. This DVD assumes you believe in divine healing and are interested in learning about specific prayer approaches and tips which have been found to increase the healing anointing.

1 session – Length: 26 Minutes

Bringing the voice of God to your learning experience

A University Without Walls

Earn an Associate, Bachelor, Master or Doctoral degree in any of these areas:

Biblical Studies
Christian Arts
Christian Counseling
Christian Entrepreneurship
Christian Leadership
Divine Healing
Intercession

Ministry
Missions & Evangelism
Prophetic Ministry
Theology
Worship Ministry
Youth Ministry

COMPLETE A SPIRIT-ANOINTED DEGREE — FROM YOUR HOME!

THE PERSONAL VALUE OF TAKING A CLU COURSE:
When you meditate on revelation truths in the context of a CLU course, you are required to fully integrate the life-changing principles. Nothing is left to chance. You will learn what you are supposed to learn and your life will be transformed by the power of the Holy Spirit.

You are invited to experience the life-transforming power of the voice of God, which is the central focus of Christian Leadership University's distance learning program. Why settle for dry education when you can, with profound consistency, receive divine revelation through every step of your educational journey?

- You can complete all coursework for your degree from home.

- Learn how to clearly hear the Lord's voice, receive divine vision, and move in the anointing of God.

- The teaching style is Hebrew rather than Greek, meaning you begin with real-life issues and, through prayerful meditation, receive enlightenment from God which results in life transformation through the power of the Holy Spirit.

- Bring in up to 50% of your degree through transcripts from other colleges, and an additional 25% of your degree through a Life Experience Portfolio.

- Total costs average $375 per course.

- Biblical, practical, spiritual, life-transforming courses.

- CLU is Evangelical, Spirit-filled and holds to the Apostles' Creed.

- Discover over 100 courses from which you may choose.

- Flexible curriculum allows you to follow your heart's desire as you take courses.

- Vocational certificates are available, composed of 10-15 courses.

- A sampling of the proven leaders who helped design your program: Ron Luce, John Arnott, Jim Goll, Mark Virkler, A. L. Gill, and Richard Booker.

Accredited by Christian Accreditation International

Christian Leadership

U N I V E R S I T Y

Bringing the voice of God to your learning experience

Are you looking for...

...a **practical**, relevant learning style that focuses on real-world problems and develops powerful, life-enhancing skills?

...a true learning *experience* where you **encounter the Holy Spirit** and receive His divine revelation on a subject?

...an **alternative** to the traditional classroom style of lectures, memorization of trivial data and rote repetition of dry facts?

...an **inexpensive, flexible** program that can be completely custom-tailored to your needs and desires?

If so, CLU is the right choice for *you*!

Call 1-800-466-6961 or
visit www.cluonline.com today

Made in the USA
Middletown, DE
23 December 2021

56722890R00133